THE
AGE
OF
SPEED

THE
AGE
OF
SPEED

LEARNING *to* THRIVE *in a*

MORE-FASTER-NOW WORLD

VINCE POSCENTE

BALLANTINE BOOKS · NEW YORK

2008 Ballantine Books Trade Paperback Edition

Copyright © 2008 by Vince Poscente

Published in the United States by Ballantine Books, an imprint of The Random
House Publishing Group, a division of Random House, Inc., New York.

BALLANTINE and colophon are registered trademarks of Random House, Inc.

Originally published in hardcover in the United States by Bard Press in 2007.

Poscente, Vince.
   The age of speed : learning to thrive in a more-faster-now world /
Vince Poscente.
      p. : ill. ; cm.
   Includes bibliographical references and index.

   ISBN: 978-0-345-50619-1
1. Success—Psychological aspects. 2. Self-management (Psychology)
3. Speed—Social aspects. 4. Quality of life. I. Title.
BF637.T5 P67 2007
158.1   2007928384

Printed in the United States of America

www.ballantinebooks.com

9 8 7 6 5 4 3 2 1

Contents

PREFACE

I have been preoccupied with speed since I was a kid just out of college, traveling around the world. The turning point for me was when a fortuneteller in Singapore told me I would die at forty—and I actually believed him.

I know it doesn't seem realistic that anybody could be that naive or fatalistic, but I guess I was particularly gullible at that age. Although I knew that the fortuneteller was most likely a fraud, the mere possibility that he could be right affected me. I worried that I might only have a few years to do all of the living I wanted to do, so I developed a peculiar and profound need to do everything fast.

Maybe I should admit another quirky thing about believing I would die at forty. It convinced me that I could not possibly die before then—and that led me to do what any immortal would: I went skydiving. I went hang gliding. I flew a sailplane. And then, when I was twenty-three, I indulged in a sport that I recommend to everyone—luge. Racing down an icy slope on your back at speeds faster than seventy miles per hour, pulling four Gs: Does it get any better than that? The speed was intoxicating, and I threw myself into the sport. I even flirted with the idea of competing in the Olympics.

Shortly after I turned twenty-six, a friend introduced me to speed skiing. More speed. More growth. More fun. And it was slated to be a demonstration sport at the Olympic Winter Games in Albertville, France, four years later. With my mortal clock ticking, I had to seize the opportunity and at least try to make it to the Olympics. Unfortunately, I had never actually competed as a skier—a detail that seemed unimportant at the time.

Before I knew it, I was thirty years old and standing on the Olympic run in the gold medal round. It had taken me, a recreational skier with no training or competition experience, only four short years to make it to the Olympics and set five Canadian national speed skiing records (216.7 kilometers per hour, or 135 miles per hour). I had gained a lot of perspective on traveling a long distance in a short time. But I only had ten years left to live, so I had to keep moving.

At thirty-three, I went on the speaking circuit as a keynote presenter. I spoke about the strategy I used to go from recreational skier to Olympic competitor in four years. I offered insights on what it takes to accomplish big goals in the shortest time possible. And I explored the role of speed in business. After earning a master's degree in organizational management, I worked with my clients, mostly Fortune 500 companies and large organizations who hired me to speak, to learn more about the ways speed affected their businesses—their bottom lines, market shares, and the success and happiness of the people who made up their organizations. In eight years, I spoke to more than seven hundred audiences, and I managed to speed into the Speaker Hall of Fame, joining the likes of Zig Ziglar, Ronald Reagan, Art Linkletter, and Og Mandino.

Everything I did was on a defined timeline, and speed was always a priority for me. Though the impetus for my preoccupation may have been silly, speed served me well. It helped me accomplish a great deal in a short amount of time and became a key factor in my success. I suppose it became a sort of secret weapon for me.

But a couple of years ago, I noticed that my fixation with speed—my secret weapon—was no longer a secret. On a mass scale, speed had penetrated the human experience. However, not everyone welcomed it with open arms. In fact, a lot of people considered the accelerated speed of life and business a problem, and that is precisely what inspired *The Age of Speed*. Now that so many people are affected by speed, I'd like to offer a new perspective to help you turn its power to your advantage and accomplish remarkable things—fast.

PART ONE

THE SPEED PHENOMENON

$$v = \frac{d}{t}$$

Chapter One

A More-Faster-Now Revolution

*I*t became clear to me that the Age of Speed was upon us while I was inching through an endless security line in the Orlando airport.

I was running late that morning, and it seemed everyone else was too—the line in front of me wrapped around twice, and it was filled with people dripping with impatience. Like them, I felt completely frustrated. I calculated that it would be at least twenty minutes before I earned the privilege of standing in my socks on the cold tile and having a stranger pat down my legs. Then I saw a woman in a business suit whisk right past the line. Carry-on in hand, she stepped to the right of the security station, paused for a moment, and continued through to the gates.

When I learned what that woman went through to save those twenty minutes, it struck me: our hunger for speed has become so acute that we are willing to sacrifice extraordinary things to satisfy it. I realized that speed is a defining characteristic of our time—that what we're experiencing is not merely the drama du jour, but a more-faster-now revolution.

The woman in the Orlando airport was a member of a registered traveler program that uses biometrics (body-scanning technology) for identification purposes. Though the word *biometrics* may not sound familiar, the concept has undoubtedly crossed your consciousness at some point—voice recognition devices, eye-scanning lasers, face recognition machines. With the help of James Bond, Charlie's Angels, and their photogenic cohorts, this is one business that has never been starved for attention. But privacy concerns and security issues have kept biometrics from becoming as widely used in real life as it is in the movies.

Ninety percent of Americans think designing safeguards against the misuse of biometric IDs is important.[1] They're concerned that biometrics presents a threat to privacy and security, both personal and national. After all, the technology identifies you based on unchangeable biological measures, and the data can be stored. Anybody with access to the stored data can read—and potentially copy—the most intimate details of your physical makeup. What if that information fell into the wrong hands? Could the police show up at your door to arrest you for a crime you didn't commit, because somebody stole your fingerprints? Could a terrorist organization use stolen data to get its members across national borders? Biometric technology makes the very constitution of our bodies vulnerable to observation, judgment, and even theft. Just how much of ourselves are we willing to reveal, to risk?

Despite this debate, Verified Identity Pass began testing its biometric identification program, Clear, in the Orlando International Airport in 2005.[2] It was as if the security and privacy concerns had become nonissues—all because VIP offered travelers the opportunity to speed up. At Orlando's airport, those registered for the Clear program wait in security lines three minutes at most, while anyone else might endure a wait of thirty-two minutes.[3] And three minutes is the maximum. According to VIP, the average wait time for Clear members is *four seconds*.

But VIP's enrollment process isn't exactly convenient or cheap, and it doesn't assuage the fears of privacy advocates, either. Before an application is sent to the Transportation Security Administration (TSA) for a security threat assessment, travelers must appear in person to undergo a background check, pay an annual fee of roughly one hundred dollars, give ten fingerprints, and submit to an iris scan.[4]

Nevertheless, the added cost, the potential compromise of personal privacy, the chore of completing the enrollment process, and the paranoia associated with being on file with the TSA proved to be no match for the lure of speed. It seems all those negatives are tolerable if it means we can go faster. By early 2007, more than forty-five thousand people had signed up for Clear nationwide, and the TSA had approved expansion of the registered traveler program in up to twenty airports.[5] Standing in the airport security line in Orlando, I bore witness as speed trumped privacy, expense, convenience, and even fear.

We are willing to make dramatic sacrifices to achieve greater speed.

The Economist summarized the situation this way: "For many people, 'biometrics' conjures images of a Big Brotherish surveillance society. But tell them they could save a few precious seconds . . . and they will sign up in the millions."[6]

FAST FACT

The Clear program is now available in San Jose, Indianapolis, Cincinnati, and British Airways Terminal 7 in New York's JFK airport. Next up: JFK Terminals 1 and 4, Newark Terminal B, and Toronto. Go to www.flyclear.com/airports.html for the most up-to-date list.

• • •

We are willing to make dramatic sacrifices to achieve greater speed because today our society pulses with new priorities and new demands. We've created a 24/7, CrackBerry, more-faster-now culture, and it is changing the way we work, relate, communicate, and live. It's changing what makes an individual successful and what makes an organization viable. And it's changing key aspects of the basic human experience.

FAST FACT

CrackBerries have become the unofficial mascot of the Age of Speed, but mind your addiction. Research revealed that allowing frequent email interruptions causes a drop in performance equivalent to losing ten IQ points—two-and-a-half times the drop seen after smoking pot.[7]

While this may seem terrifying to some, I believe speed has a unique power to enrich our lives on an individual, organizational, and even societal level. It is the lifeblood of the information age, it pushes businesses forward, and it helps people spend less time doing meaningless things to make room for more significant living.

I wrote this book to explore the possibly counterintuitive notion that when we harness the power of speed, we not only get more and get it faster, but our lives and work become less stressful, less busy, and more balanced. *The Age of Speed* is an examination of the role of speed in business and the individual experience, and a proposal for a new perspective—that speed can be a powerful ally, on both a personal and an organizational level. I will introduce you to four behavioral profiles—Jets, Bottle Rockets, Zeppelins, and Balloons—that characterize how we relate to speed, and I will help you explore ways to turn the speed phenomenon to your advantage and deal with the side effects of the Age of Speed, such as work-home interference and information overload. You'll read stories and case studies that will illustrate the many dimensions of speed's impact on our lives and businesses and also, I hope, entertain you along the way.

In many ways, *The Age of Speed* is a concept book with the humble goal of inspiring a new perspective, one that will help you thrive in this new, faster era. But the insights in this book are applicable to your life and business, and they can make a real difference. All that is required of you is an open mind and an introspective curiosity. While you read this book, consider how the content can be applied to your life and your business. And consider how speed can work to your advantage and push you closer to your goals—because speed is not only something we need to accept and embrace, but also something we desperately want.

Chapter Two

access to speed = intolerance of slow

WANT + NEED + ACCESS

*T*oday we want speed, we need speed, and we can get it—all on a level never before experienced. Of course, the human race has pursued speed for ages, but what separates our modern quest for speed from previous generations'—what makes our experience a revolution—is the combination of our ancestral desire with two factors unique to our time: an unprecedented need for speed and a new ability to achieve it. Let's first examine our desire for speed.

The degree to which we want speed today, and have wanted it for generations, is apparent in our unwavering pursuit of it. Throughout history, we have pushed to accelerate our selves, our work, and progress in general. The human race has yet to decide that our current rate of speed is, in the inspired words of Goldilocks, *just* right.

Look, for instance, at travel. Inventors, engineers, and investors have consistently challenged the time it takes to travel across the Atlantic. When transatlantic travel was confined to the sea, we sought nautical advancements—clipper ships rather than merchantmen, steamships rather than clipper ships. But even the fastest ship was not fast enough. We took to the air, and the pursuit continued. Still, even with the incredible advances made in modern aircraft, we're far from satisfied. Engineers are hard at work developing the Aerion corporate jet (scheduled to go on sale in 2011), which offers an executive and eleven companions the opportunity to travel across the Atlantic at Mach 1.5 or 1.6 at an altitude of 45,000 feet—breaking the sound barrier.[1] Imagine: morning meetings in Manhattan, a meal with clients near Piccadilly Circus, and back in time to help the kids with their homework.

FAST FACT

A Mach number is not an absolute measure of speed but a comparison of speed with the speed of sound. The speed of sound at sea level at 70° Fahrenheit is 770 miles per hour, but it changes based on atmospheric conditions such as density, temperature, and humidity. Therefore, the Mach number of a moving aircraft can vary depending on its altitude, even if it's traveling the same speed in terms of miles per hour.

But today our ability to access speed is transforming our search for it. With the boom in technology enabling us to achieve speed in almost every imaginable way, speed is no longer a luxury—it's an expectation. And the more we get, the more we seem to want. Email, PDAs, self-checkout, downloadable music, real-time news, ATMs, digital cameras: technology has driven speed into every aspect of our daily routines. The ceiling has been lifted, and our options for speeding up seem infinite. Today, we're a society of not only haves and have-nots, but also haves and have-nows. Just consider our modern consumer experience. We have valet services at malls to get into stores faster, and self-checkout kiosks to get out of stores faster. Shoppers in major metropolitan areas can even place an order as late as two o'clock in the afternoon, for anything from a cocktail dress to a book to a blender, and have it delivered *the same day*—even four days before Christmas.[2]

We crave speed, and we won't be satisfied until we get it. Our tolerance of slow has decreased as dramatically as our yearning for speed has increased. Today, wait time and downtime are considered unacceptable. Our tolerance is so low that 23 percent of Americans say they lose patience within five minutes of waiting in line.[3] Though this may seem immature and spoiled on the surface, the core of our intolerance may be rooted in something quite reasonable: Five minutes waiting is equivalent to surrendering five units of our most valued commodity—time. We've explored the potential of each minute, and we know just what we can accomplish in five. When we are forced to slow down by an external agent, we are being robbed of the things we could have accomplished in that time.

Consider what that means for businesses. There is a new standard for fast, but also a big opportunity: a widespread, deeply felt, unmet demand. People are desperate to save time—even eighteen seconds makes a difference in the Age of Speed. Chase used its ability to cut average ATM transaction time from forty-two seconds to twenty-four as a positioning strategy to appeal to the many speed seekers in its potential customer pool. Saving us a mere eighteen seconds at the ATM was enough of a selling point for Chase to launch a campaign of billboard and window displays using text-message shorthand, "Gt $ Fstr," to lure the fast and furious to its banks.[4]

And think about the offbeat car insurance provider Geico, a company determined to cash in on our zero-tolerance policy for slow. Geico used Speed Racer as a spokesperson and branded a tagline that's becoming unforgettable: "15 minutes could save you 15 percent or more." Geico's direct-to-consumer model is hardly business as usual in the slow-moving auto insurance market[5], but it works—in part by emphasizing the speed and instant gratification the model can bring customers. The company rose to fourth place in the $180 billion industry on its message of low prices and high speed, and its rivals grew worried.

One competitor tried to deliver a message that positioned it as more customer-centric, emphasizing that it would happily spend more than just fifteen minutes with customers. The company tried to appeal to a perceived consumer desire for more attention and time but eventually pulled the ad, claiming "viewers didn't get it."[6] More than likely, viewers didn't *want* it. We don't want to spend more than fifteen minutes talking about car insurance or waiting for a quote. We can no longer afford to—our time is simply too valuable. We don't just get and expect speed, we need it.

Chapter Three

SUPPLY AND DEMAND

*O*ur need for speed has become stronger, more pervasive, and harder to escape because today we can pursue more options—and we can pursue more options because our culture has flourished. According to Daniel Hamermesh, professor of economics at the University of Texas at Austin, our progress, our success, has made our time increasingly valuable. With every passing year, our minutes become more precious and more costly. "Since 1955, the average American's income after inflation has tripled . . . [while] life expectancy has gone up by roughly 10 percent."[1] So the total amount of living we can afford has tripled, while the total amount of time we have to live has increased only slightly. Therefore, we have more at stake with each minute we spend. And that has left us with an increased need for speed.

According to Hamermesh, as long as our culture continues to flourish, the need for speed will continue to become stronger, more pervasive, and harder to escape. It's a simple issue of supply and demand. There is an increased demand for time, but a virtually static supply of it. And the solution to this conflict is speed: if we cannot add more hours to the day, and the number of years in a lifetime is increasing only slightly, we have to move faster if we are to do everything we want to—and *can*—do.

Think about two kids at a state fair. Both of them have an hour to see what they want to see and do what they want to do. One child has five dollars. He has enough money to do one thing, so he has an important choice to make. Should he go on his favorite ride or buy his favorite treat? Which will provide more pleasure, the Ferris wheel or the caramel apple? Regardless of what he chooses, an hour is more than enough time to do what he can afford to do.

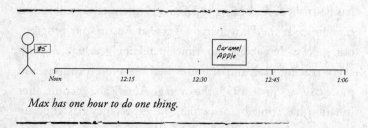

Max has one hour to do one thing.

The second child has twenty dollars—but still only an hour to spend it. She wants a caramel apple, a turkey leg, a bag of saltwater taffy, a ride on the Ferris wheel, and a ride on the Loop-the-Loop. She can afford them, but is there enough time? She can't spend too much time doing any one thing, or she'll give up the chance to do something else. A long line at the cotton candy booth could mean she misses out on the Ferris wheel. In order for her to do everything she wants to do, everything she has the potential to do, the second child has to look for ways to speed up. She has to make the most of every moment. Her need for speed is greater than the first child's.

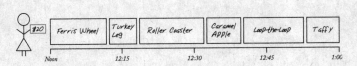

Isabella has one hour to do many things.

Like Isabella, the average American has an acute need for speed because we have the ability to pursue more options than ever before. And the more we can do, the more we want to do. Because we have finite lives and infinite imaginations, our demand for speed goes up in relation to what we have the potential to achieve. We want to do big things, meaningful things, everything we dream of. We want the extensive education, the high-powered career, the tight-knit family, the exciting social circles, the glamorous travel, the relaxed, introspective time for ourselves, and the ability to give back to our global community. And how much time do we have to cram all that into? Seventy years? Eighty? To do all that we want to

Speed is the only way
to get more time,
more life.

do, to live as much as we want to live, we need speed—it's the only way to get more time, more life.

It's true that for some people, more does not necessarily mean better. Some are perfectly content not doing everything within their reach. They choose to limit the number of experiences they pursue—and they feel happier in doing so. There is even evidence to support the notion that more does not mean happier. But, for better or for worse, if given the choice of doing less or doing more, most people feeling the effects of the Age of Speed choose more—more opportunities, more wealth, more connection to more people, more living. In fact, a 2006 poll revealed that only 26 percent of people claiming to be time starved would choose having fewer things to do over having more time to do all the things they currently do.[2] We want as much out of life as we can get.

Chapter Four

MORE LIFE, PLEASE

*T*oday, a fantastic amount of living is within reach. Not only do we have the ability to pursue more options, but we also have more options available for the pursuing. And that's the result of not only economic growth, but also technological advancement. Thanks to cell phones, remote network access, advances in travel, and the Internet, we have more options for work and more opportunities for play.

In another time, most people's options were limited to a few well-defined arenas. They could break out of those accepted roles, but there were consequences. Running away from the farm to be a painter in Paris was a *possibility*, true. But running away to Paris and still maintaining a close relationship with your mom in Iowa? Unlikely. Now, we have an unparalleled opportunity to actually do all the things we want to do. You can live in Paris and use VOIP to chat with your mom in Iowa every day. You can fly in for the holidays, and can even keep up with the local news, because you can read it online every morning.

In many cases, though, more options lead to more stress—whether we choose to pursue them or not. When we have a lot of options and many decisions to make, our destinies become less clear. Think again about the two children at the state fair. The first child, who had only five dollars, had only one decision to make. His path was clear. But the second child, who had twenty dollars, had many decisions to make. Her path was uncertain. Who do you think felt more stress?

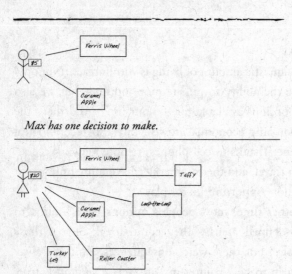

Max has one decision to make.

Isabella has a lot of decisions to make.

Barring an economic catastrophe and a sudden halt in technological development, however, the number of options available to us will not decrease anytime soon. We can certainly choose not to pursue all the options available to us, but the number of options that exist will continue to grow, regardless of our personal preferences. So ready or not, it's time to adapt to our new volume of options—and maybe even appreciate them as an opportunity to increase the amount of living we do, to increase our *quantity* of life.

With more options available, we can chase more dreams. And since we have an unprecedented ability to achieve them, we manage to catch more dreams. We may not be able to add hours to the day, but we have figured out ways to make more of each moment. The difference between what we can accomplish in sixty modern minutes and what we could do in an hour thirty years ago is astounding. Whether it's making dinner reservations, designing a complicated quarterly report, or indulging a passing fancy, we can do everything faster, so in any given minute, we can do more. We can hear a song we like on the radio, download it onto our computer, and have it on a portable player within minutes—without even standing up. In a matter of seconds, we can find answers to any question that piques our curiosity. I can send a text message to a friend and connect instantaneously—to make plans for the weekend or to say thanks for the candy-coated noodles (I have weird friends). And with a universal acronym language, programs to autocomplete words, and those handy little emoticons, even typing the message is fast.

Every time we speed up the time it takes to complete an unimportant task, we create the possibility of more time to spend doing what we feel is significant—whether it's building a business or watching the sunset. The lure of significance is a vital motivator in our rocket-powered lifestyles. We want to spend less time on things we deem inconsequential, so we devour every chance to speed up the minutiae in our lives.

Why do we need speed? Not because we'll get buried alive without it; we need it because it lets us live more meaningful lives. So why does that little voice inside us keep telling us to slow down?

PART TWO
EVOLUTION

Chapter Five

Ability to Achieve Speed

Ability to Adapt to Speed

Time

AHEAD OF OUR OWN CURVE

A few years ago, the root of our resistance to speed was revealed to me by a border collie named Scout. I was visiting a friend at his home in a suburb of Chicago when his little girl, Claire, started toward the back door to play on the swing set, away from her parents and the rest of the group. Scout blocked her way, determined to push the child back toward the crowd—or the "herd," from his perspective. Frustrated by several failed attempts to get around the dog, Claire wrinkled her nose, pushed at the furry black wall, and tried to escape. But Scout couldn't let her stray from the herd. He showed his teeth, barked, and nudged Claire hard on the shoulder. The toddler fell back on her diapered bum and started to scream. My friend came running, and Scout was sent outside in disgrace, tail between his legs. And that's when I realized why so many of us resist speed: sometimes how we behave and what we believe is based on what we've been raised to trust as true or right—not necessarily what is most appropriate and productive in our current environment.

Because border collies have been bred to herd sheep since the nineteenth century, Scout couldn't simply turn off his impulse to herd because it's an obsolete response in suburbia. And like border collies, human beings have their own ingrained responses that set them up for trouble in new environments.

Today, even when there is no clear reason to resist speed, our instincts often tell us to proceed with caution. Imagine, for example, how you would react if someone suggested that you should move faster in your life and work, that you should actively seek ways to speed up. Would you smile and feel friendly to the suggestion, or would you resist and feel stress? Think about how you would feel if you were told that today's speed of life and business isn't fast enough—that you should go even faster because if you did, you would feel less stress. What's your first reaction, acceptance or suspicion?

Outdated perspectives, irrational fears, and incongruous desires are often steering our response because negative perceptions of speed are ingrained in both our conscious and subconscious minds. That's not to say that speed is *always* the best solution, but we often try to stop speed, to slow the pace of life and business, without even considering that it could be good. It's as if we *feel* that speed is bad. For example, although I love to get things fast, there's a part of me that equates immediate gratification with childish behavior, so I feel a twinge of guilt when I consider my demand for speed. When I'm tempted to take a shortcut or try to speed up results, I'm sometimes concerned that quality or cost will suffer—that a trade-off is unavoidable. And when someone suggests that I should go faster, often I automatically interpret that to mean I'll be busier.

But if we continue to reject speed out of hand, we'll never be able to get ahead of it. We'll be in constant conflict with the world around us—a world pulsing with speed. So we need to identify the root of our resistance and work to change our view, to see speed for the positive force it can be and end our opposition. It's the first step toward thriving in the Age of Speed.

Chapter Six

NAUGHTY, NAUGHTY SPEED

Consider what we learn when we're taught the basics of right and wrong, prudent and imprudent. Even though speed is vital for success and can help us achieve great things, fast is rarely portrayed as noble, responsible, or smart. Often, it is characterized as reckless, naughty, and impatient. Wanting things fast means wanting immediate gratification, and immediate gratification is often judged as immature and irresponsible, even morally wrong. It's equated with impatience, short attention spans, and childish gimme-gimme attitudes.

Even the seemingly innocent Aesop's fable "The Tortoise and the Hare" whispers of speed's destructive potential. The moral of the story is most commonly given as "Slow and steady wins the race," with the emphasis on the dependability fast ≠ irresponsible

of slow. But like many of our societal judgments of speed, the key message of "The Tortoise and the Hare" is misguided. "Slow and steady wins the race" is a false claim based on a very limited interpretation of the story's plot.

Think about it: A tortoise and a hare agree to a race, and the hare scoots away as fast as he can go, leaving the tortoise in his dust. (Why *does* that tortoise think it's a good idea to race a hare, anyway?) But the hare is so sure the tortoise can't catch up that he stops to snack on grass and have a nap before bothering to actually complete the race. When he wakes, he sprints for the finish line. But as he dashes across, smug and sure of his victory, he finds the tortoise on the other side, patiently awaiting his arrival.

The hare doesn't lose because he's fast—speed does not work against him in any way. And the tortoise doesn't win because he is slow. The hare loses because he makes a ridiculous choice about how to spend his time, because he is irresponsible and arrogant enough to declare victory before he has finished. And the tortoise wins because he is brave enough to enter a race when the odds are stacked against him and persistent enough to make it all the way to the finish line without giving up or losing focus.

Speed's role in the fable is to exaggerate the lesson, to illustrate that even with a dramatic natural advantage—in the hare's case, speed—one must stay focused and resist underestimating the competition in order to win. On the flip side, one can win a race even against unlikely odds if she is humble, courageous, determined, and focused. Speed isn't at fault in the hare's loss, and slowness is certainly not what won the race for the tortoise. Yet generations of readers and

Why do we believe that waiting for our reward is so noble?

listeners have come away with the idea that slow is smart and fast is irresponsible.

It's true that the ability to delay gratification is one of the signs of maturity as children develop. But having mastered the skill of delaying gratification when we need to, why should we delay it on principle, for no extra benefit? And although there are some situations in which we will benefit from delaying gratification (more on that later), there's no need to dismiss it automatically as irresponsible or immature. Why do we believe that waiting for our reward is so noble? The "childish" impulse to have what you want when you want it is really no different from the reluctance to use snail mail when you can send email, to take the slow train when there's a fast one, and to beat around the bush when you want to get to the point.

But the lessons we're taught are confusing. For every story like "The Tortoise and the Hare," for every pithy quote that vilifies speed ("Haste makes waste," "Rome wasn't built in a day"), there seems to be another aphorism, another lesson, that glorifies or encourages it ("A stitch in time saves nine," "He who hesitates is lost"). And while some aspects of speed make us instinctively recoil, we're quite attracted to others.

Chapter Seven

Demand to Receive   Expectation to Give

I Hate You, but
I Want You

We've been warned of speed's potential to create problems, but we crave its benefits, so in many ways, we have a love-hate relationship with speed. We created and continue to build on the Age of Speed, but we also feel that speed is stressful, dangerous, and toxic. We lament the pace of life—the demands on our time, the expectation of availability, the feeling that we can't keep up. Many of us feel overwhelmed by the rush of life and business and strongly suspect that as speed increases, we will lose the ability to get ahead. But we've cultivated a taste for speed that pervades our society, and we're constantly developing ways to get what we want faster. So where does our pursuit of speed intersect with our distaste for it?

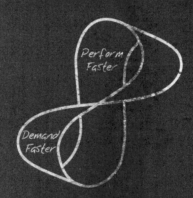

Our love of speed meets our hatred of speed at the same point that the ease of passively *receiving* meets the effort of actively *doing*. The ever-increasing demand for speed we've placed on others has come full circle. As our expectation to *get* things faster heightened, other people's expectation of us to *do* things faster also increased, so the majority of us are feeling the pressure of a seemingly sudden expectation to *do* more, to *do* fast, and to *do* now. For some reason, we didn't anticipate that. It makes sense, but we don't like it. What looks easy and exciting from the receiving end looks scary and oppressive when an external agent demands it of us: Yes, I want to get things faster, but is it okay for you to expect me to do things faster? No way!

This tension between our desire to *get* and our reluctance to *do* creates a feeling of conflict, the core of our love-hate relationship. But demand for speed is like a Möbius strip: there is only one side. We either demand it of others and accept that others will demand it of us, or we refuse speed altogether. Because if we resist going faster, producing faster, responding faster, we can't very well expect others to perform faster for us. We must accept that if we want speed in our lives, others are going to demand that we, too, speed up—that the only way to get speed is to deliver it.

Chapter Eight

fast # busy

HONEY, IT'S NOT WHAT YOU THINK

*I*f you think delivering speed means being buried beneath more work, more responsibilities, and more demands, think again. At some point, speed became tangled with busy, and that may be another reason we resist *doing* faster. If you bring up the speed of business in a conversation, chances are you'll hear someone groan and say, "I just can't go any faster. I'm too busy."

But going faster doesn't necessarily mean working harder.

In the Age of Speed, we have the tools to accomplish more in less time than our counterparts twenty years ago. Consequently, we have more time, but not necessarily more time to spend doing more work. We can use the time for things that are more important to us, things we enjoy, things that are significant.

A few months ago I was talking to two friends who are designers at an advertising agency. One started to complain about the expected turnaround time for an ad. "It actually makes me hate technology sometimes," he said. "People think that just because we can get things done faster, they can expect double the output in the same amount of time."

His coworker heartily disagreed. "I love technology. I get to spend more time coming up with ideas, and I don't have to spend days and days trying to execute them."

"But you don't get extra 'idea time' if the clients demand faster turnarounds."

"Well, even if I don't, I can still turn ads around in less time without working harder. Either way, I win."

I found this exchange interesting because it highlighted a critical issue we should consider when we resist going faster in the Age of Speed: we actually *can* do more in a given time than we could even five years ago. Therefore, the expectations we face to produce faster are often valid. But we don't have to work harder or work longer hours to accomplish more. And accomplishing more without working harder or longer translates into increased income potential—regardless of whether you're a business owner, an employee, or a freelancer. If my designer friends were freelancers, for example, they would be able to produce more designs each week, and therefore make more money each week. And since more productivity boosts profits, thrills management, and sharpens skills, salaried designers would also increase their income potential and might even be able to spend *less* time in the office. So why do people become irritated and rail against the expectation to speed up?

Perhaps it's because we don't often use the extra time for more rewarding experiences. Frequently, when we reduce the time it takes to do something insignificant, we end up using the saved time on yet another insignificant activity. If you figure out a way to save time at the bank and the grocery store, for example, do you earmark that time for something more rewarding, or do you just fill that time passively with other responsibilities that pop up? The latter scenario would leave anyone feeling exhausted, burnt out. Speed is a great solution for increasing income and productivity, but those benefits are only one piece of the picture. The bigger reason we should speed up is to make time for meaningful experiences. Speed is not just the way to get more work done—speed is the secret to having time to do what we want.

But to get the full benefit of speed, we have to detach our perception of "fast" from the notion of "busy" and become more aware of what we want to do with the time we free up. If we speed up the drudgery in our lives with a purpose in mind, we'll be more likely to fulfill that purpose and use speed as a tool for doing what we want to do, rather than doing more of everything.

Chapter Nine

SMELLING THE ROSES

*U*sing speed to live a more meaningful life is counterintuitive for most people, because speeding up means compromising the journey, missing out on smelling the roses, right? Well, not necessarily. Although this is true in some scenarios, not every experience holds deep intrinsic value. Not every experience presents us with an opportunity to develop ourselves, to make deeper connections, to find meaning. And when I suggest that you embrace speed, I'm not recommending faster strolls on the beach or accelerated games of catch with your child. I'm suggesting that you seek to speed up the minutiae in your life and work.

The key is identifying the difference between repetitive chores and passionate pursuits. We may learn useful things

the first time we complete an activity, and maybe even the second, third, and fourth time. And what we learn may make us
smarter, even wiser. But what about the twenty-third time, the
forty-eighth time, the seventy-second time? This is where the
difference—the need for speed—becomes clear. If the activity
is something you love, that you have a passion for—paint-
ing, playing music, high-level mathematics—you may want to
immerse yourself in the full experience each and every time.
But for some things in life, we should pursue speed with zeal. I
don't have a passion for grocery shopping or standing in lines,
so I really don't need to prolong those experiences. If I can
finish the chore faster by using self-checkout and get the same
result, then I should. Nor do I have a passion for cleaning my
windows or figuring my taxes, so I'm going to use every trick I
can find to speed up those jobs.

We shouldn't necessarily pursue speed in all our endeavors, but we shouldn't resist it outright under the false assumption that embracing speed means not taking time to smell the
roses. To the contrary, when we speed up the drudgery, we
have *more* time to cherish significant experiences.

But to be able to correctly gauge when speed will—and
will not—benefit us, we need to take our analysis of the value
of experiences a step further. When we think about speeding
up an activity, we need to examine whether or not the total
satisfaction in the end result will be compromised if we sacrifice the experience of anticipation. Although I believe that
immediate gratification is often a good thing and by all means
should not be rejected on principle alone, there are situations
in which delaying the prize makes the end more satisfying,

more pleasurable. MRI studies show that surges of dopamine, the brain chemical associated with pleasure and satisfaction, are linked to the anticipation of an experience more than to the actual experience.[1] So it's entirely possible that when we speed up or eliminate the time spent anticipating certain experiences, we cut the total amount of pleasure we feel. But just as not all experiences come with journeys that must be cherished, not all will result in greater pleasure if we allow time for anticipation. So in addition to asking ourselves, do I need to stop and smell the roses? we should also question whether or not we're compromising our satisfaction by sacrificing the dramatic build of anticipation. The answer may well be no, but it's worth considering.

FAST FACT

Dopamine is also linked to addictions, including addictions to sex, drugs, and even technology. Harvard psychiatrist John Ratey thinks it's at play in our compulsive use of cell phones, computers, and PDAs. In an interview with *Time* magazine, he said that if we could measure brain activity when responding to interruptions, such as incoming calls or emails, "we would probably find that the brain is pumping out little shots of dopamine to give us a buzz."[2]

Don't be fooled into
thinking that speed always
has to come at a price the
way it once might have.

———————————————

I said earlier that I don't like standing in lines, and I will do what I can to speed up that experience. But that statement is worth a second look, because not all lines are created equal. I'm willing to compromise my anticipation of, and therefore my pleasure in, the moment I buy paper towels, so I look for ways to shorten the time I spend standing in line at the grocery store. But other lines are worth waiting in because they make the end experience more rewarding. When I was a teenager, I camped out for tickets to see the Eagles in concert and stood in line for six hours. When I heard the first chord of "Hotel California," all the anticipation that had been building since the moment I got into that line culminated in a thrilling experience. I'm sure I would have enjoyed the opening song even if I hadn't stood in line for so long, but the anticipation contributed to the pleasure I felt. In this scenario, if I had sped up the time it took to acquire the tickets, I would have compromised the value of anticipation, so it was probably better not to pursue speed in that particular situation.

When choosing the best opportunities for speeding up, consider the value of both the experience leading up to the end (e.g., standing in a line) and the value of the end (e.g., paper towels or a concert). When the value of both is small, it is a good opportunity to use speed. On the other hand, when the value of one or both is significant, speed may compromise the pleasure you get from the experience. That said, don't be fooled into thinking that speed always has to come at a price the way it once might have. Times have changed in that regard.

Chapter Ten

A Love Triangle: Time, Quality, and Cost

*I*ngrained in our perception of products, services, and activities is a very basic microeconomic concept: There is a balance that must be maintained between time, quality, and cost; if you want more of one, you have to sacrifice another. It's a time-tested formula, the foundation of many decisions we make in our personal and business lives ("Fast, good, cheap: pick any two"). So as we make choices, we consider each of these variables, ranking them, assigning priority. If we have a small budget, we accept that we won't get top-notch quality. If we need superior quality, we accept that we're going to be hit hard in the wallet. And if we need something fast, it's probably going to cost more, be of lesser quality, or both. Our belief in the time-quality-cost system is based on experience: fast food is generally lousy, cheap clothing shrinks and falls apart, and buying plane tickets the day before a trip is going to cost more.

But in the Age of Speed, the rules have changed. Our demand for speed has created an environment that supports our needs and desires without requiring the sacrifices we might once have had to make. Though it is unlikely that tradeoffs between time, quality, and cost will ever cease to exist, the old tradeoff model is no longer a given. Today an incredible array of products and services allow us to pursue speed—to go faster, to get more done, to make the most of our time—without making hard decisions and resigning ourselves to "unavoidable" tradeoffs. Just consider how different shortcuts are today from those twenty years ago.

For some people, the word *shortcut* seems to evoke images of lazy people doing shoddy work. They resist shortcuts because they think the quality—or perceived quality—of the end product will be lessened. The search for shortcuts feels like an admission of a poor work ethic; shortcutters are perceived as more likely to make errors. We've all been burned at some point by trying to take a shortcut that wasn't wise or well thought out, and that experience affects our perception. We either had to accept a poor-quality product or had to redo the work, eliminating any savings in time or cost the shortcut initially offered. Haste makes waste, right?

Well, not really. Lack of focus makes waste. Poor attention to detail makes waste. I propose that taking shortcuts can actually be beneficial, because a shortcut can be a faster, more efficient way to achieve an end. And if taking a shortcut enables us to be more focused on the aspects of a project that require our utmost attention, then it can improve the quality of the end result. I am not saying that all shortcuts are good (surgeons probably shouldn't take too many), just that we should not reject them out of hand.

Because of technology, we have more shortcuts available to us than ever before—and this new brand of shortcut not only saves us time, but often also saves us money and produces equal or better quality. For example, think about the difference between taking a shortcut when making airline reservations twenty years ago and taking one today. In the '80s, a typical shortcut would be calling only one airline to buy a ticket rather than calling around to shop for the best price. It might have saved time, but unless the one call just happened to be the airline with the best fare, the shortcut cost us money. Today, the most common shortcut is to skip the phone calls and jump onto a travel website such as Travelocity.com or Expedia.com. Within minutes, we can have a reservation booked and a confirmation in our email inbox. And since travel websites present us with a comprehensive list of flight options from multiple airlines sorted by price, as well as discounted rates often available exclusively online, we also save money. On top of that, we experience no compromise in quality—we end up flying in the same kind of plane we would've flown in if we had picked up the phone and called a ticket agent. Some may even argue that quality goes up because the customer experience is more satisfying when the process is simpler, we have more options, and we save time and money. Nevertheless, the notion that speed leads to a more pleasant, less stressful experience is contrary to what most people believe. Maybe it's time to change that—maybe it's time to embrace speed.

Chapter Eleven

BREAKING UP
WITH RESISTANCE

At this fork in the road, I can't help but draw connections to the way we reacted in the '90s when technology first blew through our offices, homes, and communities. Seemingly overnight, we were faced with an unprecedented degree of *change*. And just as *speed* affects us on a personal, emotional level today, in the '90s change created high tension, emotional resistance, and acute discomfort in businesses and homes.

Of course, the agent of all this change was the tech boom—it took hold of our stock portfolios, our business models, and our personal lives. Techies (a social order that seemed to break into the mainstream overnight and then multiply like gremlins) led us onto the "information superhighway" and things started to come undone. Suddenly we all had to learn how to interact with and use computers, cell phones, and lots of things that went *beep* and had us crawling under desks to plug in chargers. Everyone needed skills previously reserved for engineers, scientists, and a passionate fringe culture. As societal and professional standards started to morph, concepts such as *smart* and *successful* were redefined. Age, education, social savvy, and experience gave way to technical savvy, creativity, and the ability to adapt and learn new things.

Even our way of communicating was turned upside down. Successful executives, lawyers, and doctors who hadn't typed in ages were suddenly facing a communication infrastructure based on email. Our vocabulary changed to a degree never before experienced. Seemingly overnight, words and acronyms that had meant nothing to us the day before were popping up in casual conversation. Words we had known since childhood had been repurposed. (If a friend told me he had a worm in 1997, it meant something very different from what it would have meant in 1987. And who would've guessed that *pirates* would be making headlines in 1999?)

The change movement pushed us into a constant state of learning, which proved to be too much for some people. Talk of the "digital divide" permeated everyday conversation, the media, and professional conferences. Everyone felt the pressure, but not everyone was ready or willing to adapt. Some of us didn't want to start carrying a cell phone. Some of us didn't want a computer at home. And some of us liked the way things were, before the Internet and before email—when spam was an innocent can of processed meat and "backing up" referred to the immediate need to call a plumber.

But just as speed shows no signs of letting up now, change dug in its heels and demanded recognition. And just as familiarity breeds contempt, inevitability breeds acceptance. We had to respond—to stop resisting—or face obsolescence. Business models changed from top-down, vertical structures to more individualistic, horizontal institutions. Employees in the new system began to understand that companies, jobs, and economies were unstable, and that in order to safeguard their lifestyles, they needed to safeguard their marketability. *Change*, *flexibility*, and *lifelong learning* became buzzwords. And then we reached a turning point.

Shortly after recognition spread, a movement grew to accept change. Thought leaders like John Kotter popularized the notion that change could be a good thing. That it could be so good, in fact, that we should not only accept it, but also seek to create it. Kotter released *Leading Change* in 1996, establishing a dichotomy between management and leadership based on the concept that management is mostly concerned with the status quo, while leadership is tied to change. And Spencer Johnson's *Who Moved My Cheese?*, a parable on how to deal with change through optimism, self-awareness, and flexibility, followed two years later and went on to become a number-one international bestseller with more than ten million copies in print after two years.[1] Businesses and individuals adopted a new perspective on change, realizing that if change is here to stay, it might be a good idea to embrace it.

This mentality of welcoming change and using it to our advantage began to change our environment. The change movement, through technology and globalization, renewed the economy and revolutionized our relationships with the outside world, individually and collectively. A global market of sources and customers is now necessary to the functioning of business.

The sheer penetration of technology illustrates our remarkable acceptance of change. In 2006, *Computerworld* noted, "If all PCs had gone dark 20 years ago, you could have gone back to your typewriter and done pretty much the same work. If the entire Internet had shut down 10 years ago, the effect on business would have been negligible. Today, either of these events would bring business to a standstill."[2]

The new world of change assembled itself within a decade. In the next ten years, the same thing will happen again—only this time the revolution is speed. Culture, business, and the individual experience are undergoing another major shift— one that is equally powerful and has the potential to be equally positive. If we can accept the positive potential that speed offers, we can do more, be more, live more. The change movement is a template that can guide us through the Age of Speed: rather than bucking speed, vowing to find solutions for moderating it, we should embrace it and find ways to create more of it.

Our resistance to speed was motivated by forces that have undergone dramatic change in recent years.[3] Not all the values we once had to apply to the concept of speed are relevant. Though we have been taught that if we embrace speed, we will be forced to compromise quality, cost, our values, and our peace of mind, those rules don't necessarily apply in the Age of Speed—and when they do apply, we don't have to reject speed outright, we simply have to be more mindful of the value of our experiences. We no longer have to assume that we will always have to compromise when we make speed a priority. We don't have to assume that if we embrace speed, our lives will just get busier and busier. We're in a new environment, a new game, and we need to play by different rules. We need to adapt, evolve, and shed our outdated or misguided perceptions of speed. We need to reshape the way we define, manage, and categorize our time.

PART THREE

THE BIG BLUR

Chapter Twelve

OUT OF BOUNDS

Since time is scarce in the Age of Speed, more and more people are struggling to balance work and home, but my friend Ann has it all together. Despite being a successful intellectual property attorney and mother of two, she has no problem shielding her leisure time and home life from work invasion. After dropping the kids off at school, Ann gets to work at the same time every morning. At the office, she spends her morning taking care of her clients' and associates' needs, so when she goes to lunch, she doesn't even think about work. She dines with a friend or eats alone and reads a novel. In the afternoon, she completes the rest of her scheduled responsibilities—one hour for client calls, one hour for emails, two hours for casework. She leaves the office at 5 PM every day and totally disconnects: when she gets home, all of her time and attention is focused on her family, her hobbies, and relaxation.

There's only one problem with this story: it's not true. Ann dreams of this life, but it's not her reality. You're about as likely to meet a successful professional with a life like the one I just described as you are to put the jelly on first when you make a PB&J sandwich. (Seriously, that's very rare. Ninety-six percent of people start with the peanut butter.[1] Now, aren't you glad you bought this book?) Like most people in the Age of Speed, my friend Ann feels exhausted, pulled in opposing directions, ripped at the seams. Taking her kids to school often means she gets into the office later than she'd like when one of them loses a backpack or forgets his lunch. Her clients and associates need things all day long, not just in the morning, and they often interrupt her while she's trying to make it through her casework or emails. Sometimes she ends up working late into the evening or answering email from home. She feels guilty and thinks she's neglecting her family and becoming a workaholic, but it's hard to turn off. Ann suffers from one of the most common side effects of the Age of Speed: blurred boundaries between work and home.

One reason for the blur is that disconnection is becoming extinct at a phenomenal rate. Technology continually becomes faster, smaller, cheaper, and more portable, so we're staying more and more connected to our work when we're at home or having fun. Although work no longer keeps us chained to desks or even desktops, we're experiencing an "always-on" phenomenon—whether it's an email, text message, instant message, or cell phone call, we're almost always accessible.

FAST FACT

In 2006, Hyatt hotels began to offer a special arm, hand, and thumb massage to cater to the aches of the PDA-toting crowd. The special service is known as "BlackBerry Balm."[2]

As network technology advances and cell phones, PDAs, laptops, and the like become more available and user-friendly, our relationship with time—the way we define it, manage it, and use it—has changed dramatically. Now that we can be in almost constant contact with friends and family, have immediate access to an incredible array of entertainment, and conduct business remotely from anywhere (in a plane, on a train, or in bed), traditional definitions of time, like our traditional perceptions of speed, are becoming obsolete.

The big blur between free time and work time makes us feel that our overall time is compromised, that it isn't ours to control. No matter how fast we think we're going, it seems harder and harder to dedicate time to the things we feel are significant—whether that's family, customers, philanthropy, or any other pursuit. But I blame this problem partly on the outdated framework we use to delineate and organize our time. We define our time in discrete segments—work, home, and leisure—but that's no longer accurate. Now, like Ann, most of us deal with constant overlap and unclear priorities.

This problem can be traced back to when we shifted from an agricultural society to an industrial one, when people started to define their time according to the place where they spent it. No longer only something people did, work became a place people went. As a result, time has been associated with physical boundaries for more than a century.[3] After all that time, we got used to the idea that we work when we are in the office or at the factory. We do chores when we are in the kitchen. We relax when we are in the living room or at the park.

This made time easy to define, simple to understand. It made time controllable. If we felt too much stress or believed our work was encroaching on our leisure time, the answer was simply to scale back the amount of time spent at work and increase the amount of time spent at home or wherever we went for fun and relaxation. Our decision was based on a simple option: Be at location X less and location Y more. There may have been more complex aspects to the decision (what did we need to do to allow us to spend less time at work?), but the basic solution was straightforward.

Today, however, work is no longer a place—it's a state of mind. The spatial and task-oriented boundaries that once dictated how we spent our time have become blurred, almost invisible. And instead of three distinct segments of time, we have ended up with one large pie of time filled with a constantly morphing mixture of work, home, and leisure.

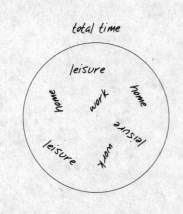

The framework that gave us discipline over our time and kept work in a neat little box has been rendered obsolete.

But I propose that if we define a new alternative to the work-home-leisure model, we will be able to take advantage of all of the opportunities available to us today more easily, and we will feel the benefits of an evolved way of life. We will not only quell the pain of the most common side effect of the Age of Speed (blurred boundaries between work and home), but also establish an individual purpose for speeding up, a way to use the time we save on the things that matter most to us.

Chapter Thirteen

MAKING A NEW PIE

Yvon Chouinard, the founder and CEO of outdoor gear and apparel company Patagonia, often tells the story of a trip he took with the leaders of his company to South America—to the *real* Patagonia. The company had experienced phenomenal growth in the mid-1980s, but the recession at the end of the decade hit them hard. In a tough spot, they had to do something radical, so they headed to Argentina and climbed a mountain. (No conference rooms for these adventurers.) When they reached the top of the mountain, they didn't talk about what strategy they needed to employ to get their bottom line back on track; they talked about their vision for an ideal future—not what they *had* to do, what they *wanted* to do. They knew that if they went back to their roots, their passion, they could solve the problems they faced. Chouinard names several principles he and his team outlined on that trip, but one in particular caught my attention.

The Patagonia team realized that in their ideal company, there was no separation between work and home or leisure. They believed that they should enjoy the eight to ten hours a day at work as much or more than the other hours of their lives. They didn't think they should have to redefine their values and passion during business hours. And if their values didn't change from hour to hour or from Sunday to Monday, why should the way they focused their time—all of their time?

Of course, this wasn't the first time I had heard the notion of blending work and pleasure, but Chouinard's story planted an idea in my brain: this is precisely what we need to resolve the issue that's leaving people torn between work and home in the time-starved Age of Speed. The solution he found is the evolved context we ought to apply to replace the outdated work-home-leisure time model.

Chouinard and his staff at Patagonia don't look for new ways to keep work out of their personal time—they look for ways to put personal time and passion into their work. Their time is organized and structured according to what they value, what brings them joy—not the physical space they're occupying or the particular task they're doing. Rather than thinking of their time as divided between work, home, and leisure, they think of it as a resource offering opportunities to explore their values and accomplish their goals. And it works: today, Patagonia, which is still privately owned, pulls in roughly a quarter of a billion dollars a year in gross revenue.

FAST FACT

Headquartered on the California coast, Patagonia has a policy that employees who hang ten are free to leave work when the surf's up. The ocean doesn't follow business hours, so Chouinard sees no reason why surfers who work for Patagonia should have to miss the waves Monday through Friday.

To understand the evolution, consider that if an office worker of the 1950s diagrammed his time in a pie chart, it would probably look like the traditional definition of time as illustrated on page 68. Now contrast this with what Chouinard's pie chart might look like: the segments would probably be values-based.

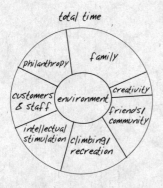

In the Age of Speed, our
time is more fluid—
and that should be
working in our favor.

When we stop applying the work-home-leisure framework to our time and start applying a framework based on values, we shift from a choked perspective focused on spatial context and tasks to an open, conscious perspective based on what we value and what we want to accomplish. In the Age of Speed, our time is more fluid—and that should be working in our favor, not making us feel stressed out and exhausted.

In the same way that we can respond to a client's need with lightning-fast speed from the couch, we can send pictures of our families to relatives while we're at work. Parents can work from home when their kids get sick, and friends can text message each other the moment a plane lands to schedule a visit during a business trip. We can integrate home and leisure into our work, just as work has become integrated into our home and leisure time. Time can be a single powerful resource that we use to accomplish our goals and dreams, regardless of where we are.

When we implement the values-based time model in our lives, time becomes the tool we use to organize our priorities and values rather than our duties and location—how we spend our time reflects who we are rather than where we are or what we're doing. It's not a question of how much you have to do or how fast you're going, it's a question of whether or not the way you spend your time is in line with your values and goals.

FAST FACT

Jonathan Schwartz, the CEO of Sun Micro-systems, told a reporter at *Fortune*, "There is no line between personal life and professional life, especially if you care a lot about what you do. I used to really resent that, and then it became really freeing."[1]

The benefits of this new model are not limited to the individual, either. There is a growing trend among companies to promote boundary-free time for both employee development and bottom-line results. Best Buy, through its Results-Only Work Environment (ROWE), allows employees the freedom to decide where, when, and how they work—as long as they get the job done. Best Buy has moved far beyond the typical approach to flextime—allowing employees to start and end their days around a core set of hours—and encourages employees to break all the rules of standard business operating procedure. It's no longer about how many hours you spend in the office; it's all about productivity and outcomes. This leads to a totally different evaluation of how you spend your time. According to Cali Ressler, a consultant and former employee who helps manage the program, "'You start looking at everything and saying, is this really going to help get me to my desired outcome? Pretty soon you've cut out ten of those unnecessary things that used to fill up your week, and you're getting a lot more done.'"[2] Employees regularly call in to meetings rather than attend in person, work late at night when they know their counterparts in other countries are awake, and take long lunches or walks in the park on beautiful days.

But ROWE is more than just a new type of flextime program; it's a complete about-face for business operations, from both the employer and employee perspective. Jody Thompson, a former employee and Ressler's partner, described the immensity of the change: "'Basically, we're rewiring people's brains, getting rid of an old belief system from the 1950s that is no longer relevant to the technologically advanced business world we have now. We want people to stop thinking of work as someplace you *go to*, five days a week from 8 to 5, and start thinking of work as something you *do*.'"[3]

The benefits are remarkable. Employees in divisions that are part of ROWE report that their family relationships, company loyalty, and focus on their work have all improved since the program began.[4] And the results are affecting the bottom line, too. Surveys have shown a 35 percent increase in productivity for employees working in the ROWE program. Estimates indicate that the company will save as much as $13 million per year in turnover costs once all four thousand corporate employees are converted to the program. Perhaps Steve Hance, employee relations manager, said it best: "'I used to schedule my life around my work. Now I schedule my work around my life.'"[5]

If we stop judging our time according to outdated definitions of work, home, and leisure, we are less likely to feel stressed out about the blurred lines. If we stop forcing the separation between those three areas of our lives, we won't suffer when they merge—instead, we'll find solutions. If we're emailing a customer from the couch at eight o'clock at night, we shouldn't be asking the question, am I working during family time? Since many of us work at home now, the answer to this question will not address the real issue—and with no practical way to separate home from work, the question just adds stress and anxiety. We should be asking, is the total time I've spent with my family today (or this week) in line with how much I value time with my family? If the answer is yes, we can feel at peace with our choice to send the email. If the answer is no, and we've been spending too much time with customers at the expense of family, we have a variety of options to change the balance: spend more time on work tasks when our families aren't available, examine other pieces of the pie to ensure that we haven't spent more time on another valued endeavor at the expense of work, and so on. No more stress from intrusions and interruptions, no more doubts about misplaced priorities, no more resentment of our loss of control over our own time.

Think again about Patagonia's Yvon Chouinard. Regardless of whether he is at home, in the office, or on a mountaintop, he spends time protecting the environment. He spends time nurturing his family. He spends time developing Patagonia. And when he's on a conference call from home, his home life isn't taking a back seat to his work and his work isn't taking a back seat to his home life. His time is one cohesive resource that he invests in multiple values.

Although the work-home-leisure model was once a good tool for prioritizing our time and balancing our values, it doesn't fit in our new environment. The values-based framework that has evolved lets us organize our time according to priorities with a more expansive perspective—a perspective big enough for the Age of Speed. It relieves the stress of having to separate our time into work, home, and leisure, constantly battling interference, and it gives us the freedom to pursue our values and indulge our passions at any time of the day.

Of course, not everyone can apply the values-based model on the same scale as Best Buy or Patagonia. After all, some people get paid by the hour and so have no choice but to tie work to precise hours and locations. Others are in roles that allow little freedom for pursuing any personal interests during work time. If you're not a business owner or in a role that can affect change on an organizational level, you may feel that you can't organize your time according to your values because you have to organize it according to your boss's. But the values-based model works on a smaller scale, too—even if there are limits to how much of your schedule you can redesign.

Regardless of your work situation, shifting your perspective of time from a focus on tasks and physical location to a focus on values can help you deal with the daily pressures common in the Age of Speed. The values-based model solution is an exercise in consciousness—an awareness of your values. All that is required is some thoughtful adaptation. Ask yourself, how can I explore the things I find meaningful while I work? In my doctor's office, a nurse once told me that his mission in life was to "bring people joy." He focused his time—both on and off the job—on doing just that. Whenever I'm there, I can hear him singing down the hall before he walks into the room—and there's always a trail of laughter and happy voices following him. He is blending his work time with his personal values. And it makes him happier and more productive. Some people will be able to blend personal and professional time more easily than others, but even a small change can have a profound impact on your life.

Chapter Fourteen

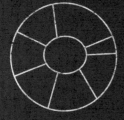

DEFINING OUR PIE

*I*n order to apply this new context to time, to change the perspective that defines our relationship with speed, we have to spend time thinking about how we spend our time. If we shake off the work-home-leisure context, we need to replace it with something that helps us organize our time and make the most of every hour.

First, we have to examine the *why*—the reason behind the rush. We need to take the time to think about what we want to do with the time we create by speeding up the minutiae, applying speed to the trivial things in life. When we identify why we're speeding up, speed itself will carry more significance in our lives—it will assume the value it deserves.

Next, we should consider the *what*—what values belong in our pie, how we want to spend our hours, our days. This new framework doesn't have a one-size-fits-all solution. Unlike the work-home-leisure template, the values-based model requires some contemplation. My time should be organized according to how much I value family, how much I value my work, how much I value introspective alone time, friends, wealth, the environment, politics, and various social issues. And once we define our pies, we should refer to them often, objectively considering whether or not the way we spend our time reflects what we value.

With a focus on what value each task is serving, rather than on the task itself, you can make the most of your scarce time—and you can successfully manage your priorities. You can have a better understanding of how you use your time to support your values, and you can make adjustments based on more comprehensive, more relevant assessments.

The new model forces us to consider what we value and whether our behavior is aligned with those values. It broadens our perspectives and offers opportunities to lead examined lives with less stress, more direction, and greater potential to thrive. It is an active, responsible approach to living in an era with diminished boundaries between work, home, and leisure. The values-based framework will help us make speed work for us—help us see that far from being just another metric to improve, speed is a tool for achieving more significance and accomplishing more of the goals that matter to each of us.

But to live a life of meaning and significance, we need more than just a new perspective—we need enough time to support all of our values. In other words, we need speed. After all, the life spent valuing family, friends, wealth, and intellectual growth is probably more fulfilling than the one chasing only wealth and intellectual growth, but the richer life also requires more time. If we want to use our hours and days to further our big goals, we need to use speed to create enough time to pursue more than just work tasks and mundane duties.

PART FOUR

FOUR PROFILES

Chapter Fifteen

SPEED, SUCCESS, AND FAILURE

My daughter Alex had a hard time learning how to ride a two-wheeler. She insisted on doing it by herself, and the process was a long one with an impressive number of skinned knees. But I remember the day she finally had a breakthrough.

She was taking it slow so she wouldn't crash and get hurt once again, but she couldn't seem to keep her balance. The bike's wheels wobbled and she swerved wildly to keep herself upright as she tilted first left, then right. I saw her starting to fall, and I tensed, ready to run to her rescue. Then, in a last-ditch effort to stay upright, she started pedaling faster.

Suddenly the bike was moving in a straight line, no more crazy swerves or wobbles. As soon as Alex sped up, everything got a lot simpler. She got into a rhythm, keeping a fast, steady pace. She easily avoided a rock in her path, and cruised down the sidewalk as if she'd been riding for years. But then things took a turn for the worse. In her excitement, she looked over at me with a big proud smile. She was riding fast, but not looking in the direction she was headed—which, unfortunately, was straight into a parked car. She walked away from the ordeal with a few bruises, but she had discovered some valuable insights.

Once Alex sped up, she found she could maintain her balance by making small corrections as she rode, instead of having to constantly jerk the handlebars from side to side. Speed helped stabilize the bike. She could swerve around obstacles in her path without panicking and falling over—staying upright was infinitely easier. She discovered that the key to a smooth, sure ride is getting your speed up to the point where you're in control and looking at the road ahead, not wobbling desperately and staring at your wheels. Alex learned that resisting speed led to failure, whereas embracing speed made the ride effortless and successful—until she lost focus and control.

Watching Alex at first fail, then succeed as she learned to embrace speed, I thought about how the same principles translate into the success or failure of businesses and individuals in the Age of Speed. When you're riding a two-wheeler, you're in an environment that sets a minimum speed for success. Many individuals and businesses today find themselves in a similar situation. But embracing speed was not enough to keep Alex on the bike. It got her past the first round of obstacles, but she had to do more to avoid crashing into the car. Today, the same is true for people and businesses striving for success. If you're in an environment that requires speed, you must embrace it.

And if you embrace it, you must know what it takes to succeed at top speeds, so you don't crash.

Evaluating these three core issues—whether speed is embraced or resisted, whether it is required in a specific environment or irrelevant, and whether it works for or against the person or organization in question—I noticed that four behavior patterns have emerged in the Age of Speed. To describe them, I'm going to introduce you to four profiles: Zeppelins, Balloons, Bottle Rockets, and Jets. Together, they fit into a two-by-two grid:

	Resist Speed	Embrace Speed
Succeed	Balloons	Jets
Fail	Zeppelins	Bottle Rockets

Once you get to know them, you'll recognize the behaviors that categorize these profiles everywhere you look—in your colleagues, your family, your company, the receptionist at your dentist's office, the talking heads on TV. You may even recognize your own behavior patterns.

Chapter Sixteen

ZEPPELINS

*H*ave you ever worked with or for a company that required five, seven, or even eleven levels of approval for the simplest initiative or communication? Have you ever wondered how a company has survived as long as it has by relying on slow, archaic methods for communication, data gathering, and customer service? Have you ever sat in a meeting, forced to listen as someone complains about how fast changes are made or how it is impossible to go faster, unreasonable to even explore the possibility?

You've probably been touched by a Zeppelin, and chances are good that you came away from the encounter trying not to scream in frustration. Zeppelins aren't trying to make you crazy. It's just their instinctive response to the speed they see coming for them—resist, resist, resist. The fact that their resistance is futile is lost on them. They don't see any other choice.

Zeppelins can't fly fast
enough or soar high enough
for the Age of Speed.

Zeppelins proceed at a slothlike pace and have a tough time maneuvering or changing course quickly. Zeppelins are lagging and lumbering, dangerous and potentially explosive—and like the notorious Hindenburg, they face inevitable failure. Today, they are obsolete: Zeppelins can't fly fast enough or soar high enough for the Age of Speed.[1]

FAST FACT

Thirty-six people died when the 804-foot Hindenburg exploded and crashed into the ground in 1937. It was filled with more than seven million cubic feet of hydrogen.[2]

Zeppelins see speed approaching and feel threatened or angry. They see no way to go faster. They can't understand why anyone would *want* to speed up. They see speed as a harbinger of impending doom: greater stress, more work, chaos. They're blind to the world of options and opportunities that speed offers.

Of course, that doesn't usually lead to success and happiness. Zeppelins commonly feel rushed, stressed out, not in control of their own lives. They're continually hitting the brakes, but nothing happens—the world around them whooshes by at an ever-increasing pace. Everyone makes demands of them that they just *know* they can't meet. The only option for taking control, at least according to Zeppelins, is to slow down. So Zeppelins build walls between themselves and speed in all its forms. They simply don't demand speed. They resist adopting technology that can help them speed up. They rarely use the Internet, whether to shop, explore, or find answers to basic questions. If they need something fast, they feel sure they'll have to sacrifice something for speed. They'd rather take their time, whatever the cost.

As we might expect from any approach rooted in resistance, Zeppelin tendencies are dangerous to businesses. Look, for instance, at Eastman Kodak—a strong, profitable, and innovative company throughout the twentieth century that has not fared well in the twenty-first. One of their biggest problems was their failure to embrace speed in an environment that demanded it.

Even though Kodak invented the digital camera in 1994 and had brand name recognition that could have made it a powerhouse in the early digital market, it proved to be too slow for its environment. Although the company was theoretically following a ten-year plan to gradually shift to digital technology, little was actually changing.[3] It wasn't until 2000 that Kodak threw its weight behind the digital revolution.

Like other Zeppelins, Kodak actively resisted speed even though its environment demanded it. So in 2000, its late entry into the fight for market share was reactive and precautionary. Instead of capitalizing on consumers' positive response to the speed of digital cameras, Kodak launched its digital camera program as a just-in-case option while continuing to focus on its slowing film business, trying to lure customers back with aggressive marketing.[4] But as digital cameras continued to improve and get cheaper, consumers were no longer willing to wait to get film developed, and no amount of marketing could hold back the shift.

Kodak's user-friendly innovations eventually earned it a larger share of the digital camera market, but by then commoditization and competition had sliced margins. Kodak could have had first-mover advantage, but it lost that opportunity due to slow reaction time and delayed recognition of the digital threat.[5] Huge losses on the film side dragged down the modest profits from late digital success, and the company posted continual losses from the third quarter of 2004 to the same quarter two years later. In one quarter alone, Kodak lost $37 million.[6]

Kodak's CEO, Antonio Perez, promoted to the post in 2003, recognized the company's resistance to speed and has a plan he thinks can put it back in the black by the end of 2007. Perez says he is fighting Kodak's ingrained tendency "'to test a new product or service—and then test and test again to make it perfect, even if it stretches out the journey to the marketplace'"[7]—even if the incremental result, in terms of quality, doesn't justify taking the additional time. Kodak has traditionally ignored the benefits of speed, but Perez's philosophy emphasizes embracing speed and the opportunities it offers: one of his seven notions of innovation is "Speed is critical, so push your company."[8]

Although Kodak has a long haul ahead of it, the company's newest offerings show promise. If it can get to market fast enough, Kodak may emerge from its Zeppelin past as a faster company with potential to thrive in the Age of Speed.

Chapter Seventeen

BALLOONS

*B*alloons are the happy individuals and successful organizations that don't seek speed and don't need to: mountaintop gurus, perfume testers, the small business that makes handcrafted collector's items. You may find the occasional Balloon in an office job, but it's probably the rare position in which she can proceed at her own pace and won't fail by resisting speed. But in general, Balloons have chosen to live outside the Age of Speed. Instead, they seek or create environments in which there are few external pressures demanding that they speed up. They interact with our fast culture only from a distance.

Where Zeppelins like Kodak resist speed and face inevitable failure, Balloons resist speed but find success. Like their namesake—the hot-air balloon—these resistors float along, content to reach a general destination eventually. They can change their environment the way a hot-air balloon can change

Balloons often inhabit niche markets, where their specialized skills are valued regardless of the time they cost.

its altitude, so they can avoid situations that require them to move at speeds faster than they are comfortable with. They don't lack purpose; it's just that their purpose, like enjoying the view from above, has little to do with speed.

FAST FACT

It's possible that the first version of the hot-air balloon was made out of an eggshell in second-century-B.C. China. In *The Ten Thousand Infallible Arts of the Prince of Huai-Nan*, the author wrote, "Eggs can be made to fly in the air by the aid of burning tinder." The Chinese would remove the contents from an eggshell, then light a weed on fire inside the hole of the shell to reduce air density inside and make the shell fly.[1]

This seemingly simple detachment from the spirit of the age is a hard thing to come by. Balloons can't exist in most industries today. They often inhabit niche markets, where their specialized skills are valued regardless of the time they cost. Their work fulfills and engages them, and they do it well. They find success primarily because they aren't actively resisting speed, putting themselves in its path and trying to erect a barricade. Their resistance is really more a form of avoidance.

Balloons aren't up on the most recent technological advances; you're not likely to meet one with much use for a

BlackBerry. Their needs are more focused on ease and comfort than productivity, so they consume speed only in the ways that make their lives and work simpler.

In their general detachment from speed, Balloons give up some of their potential, some of their opportunities. But they make the sacrifice mindfully. Remember the kids at the fair? Balloons are like the second child in that they, too, have twenty dollars, but they would choose to ride only one ride or eat one treat. To protect their lives and businesses from the effects of speed, they limit the number of options they pursue—they choose to do less despite their potential to do more. They avoid expanding their businesses once they reach a sustainable level. They often don't seek promotions or other forms of advancement—they're satisfied, content. For the most part, they maintain their status quo. Things will speed up over time, but Balloons are snugly ensconced in their protected worlds and don't worry much about when. They've looked at the choices and have chosen a path with limits over a path with speed.

Because they're almost always conscious of their choice and have sought out an environment that supports that choice, it usually works out well for them. Take the example of the once fast-tracked Zinn Cycles, maker of custom bicycles for hardcore cyclists.

In the mid-90s, Zinn Cycles began expanding rapidly. The company took on more and more employees, worked with sales representatives, and sold standard models to bike shops. For success in the mass-market retail world, speed was vital, and Zinn Cycles was on a roll. But founder Lennard Zinn wasn't happy. The stress of producing more and more and expanding faster and faster proved to be the wrong track for this Balloon. "What I found was that I hardly rode my bike anymore, and the whole reason I do this is because I love bike riding. For me that was too high a cost to pay. I wasn't willing to sacrifice that for a business."[2]

So he changed his environment to one that doesn't demand speed: He bought out his partner, helped his employees start their own businesses, and became a one-man shop producing only custom bikes. The company has fewer customers now and a cap on its earning potential, but Lennard Zinn is again riding his bike to work every day, and that makes him happy.

Balloons are rare, and that's because most environments today *do* demand speed. If you're in an environment that demands speed, you cannot succeed as a Balloon. Instead, you'll face the fate of the Zeppelin: inevitable obsolescence or explosion. So it would seem that if you embrace speed, you'll be sure to find success, right? Unfortunately, it's not quite that simple.

Chapter Eighteen

BOTTLE ROCKETS

*E*mbracing speed and viewing time as a valuable resource for achieving our goals will help us succeed in our more-faster-now world. But it takes more than that to harness the power of speed, to make it work *for* us—as the case of the Bottle Rocket shows us.

You can easily identify a Bottle Rocket: The friend who speeds through traffic and rushes from appointment to appointment, but takes on so many responsibilities that she never manages to get ahead. The endlessly energetic coworker who powers through the day at top speed, throwing out ideas at random while checking email and talking on the phone—always moving fast, but never managing to achieve anything of substance. The company that takes off and embraces speed at every turn, but either loses sight of its goals and fails to reach its once-glorious potential or stays stubbornly focused on the wrong path. All of them are going just as fast as they can, propelled through life at a breakneck pace, leaving notes and ideas swirling in their wakes. For all the energy and enthusiasm they pour into everything they do, they rarely achieve sustainable, long-term success.

Bottle Rockets pursue speed at all costs, but their inability to use speed to their advantage makes them dangerously explosive. They may be going fast, but they aren't doing it in a smart way. Their efforts aren't always aligned with a clear destination, so they struggle to stay on a healthy course. They can't turn to respond to changes in their environment. Sometimes their paths become wildly unpredictable, their speed goes out of control, and they end up diving straight into the ground.

FAST FACT

The Chinese invented bottle rockets in the thirteenth century as a weapon—and they're still highly dangerous. A modern Class C bottle rocket can take off at seventy-five miles per hour.[1]

Bottle Rockets are devoted to speed—they embrace it in all things and their demand for it is high. They'll adopt any new technology that offers to speed things up, but they won't take the time to learn how to use the aspects of the new technology that make it so beneficial. They assume speed will always be available to them, so they do most things on the spur of the moment or at the last minute and are disappointed when the results aren't exactly what they envisioned.

Lacking agility, Bottle Rocket companies have difficulty adjusting to new standards or practices, to new ideas and developments in their industry. Often their speed is wasted on the wrong outlets or lost in pointless, unexamined procedures. They're so focused on going fast, they don't take time to understand why they're going fast, where they're trying to go, or what might be holding them back. Once a company is set on a Bottle Rocket path, it experiences stop-start progress and unpredictable waves of viability. At worst, it simply self-destructs.

FAST FACT

Not so easy on the eyes, those bottle rockets. The real ones cause 100 percent of the firework injuries that result in having an eye surgically removed.[2]

What's so destructive about the way Bottle Rockets seek speed? Like their namesake, Bottle Rockets are explosive and uncontrollable. They go fast, but don't change direction or stop—until they reach the point where they finally explode or fizzle and plummet to the ground. The trajectory they follow doesn't necessarily lead to their true calling—nor to fast results. Our metaphorical Bottle Rockets lack one or all of the critical characteristics—aerodynamics, agility, and alignment—that would give them the ability to harness the power of the speed they chase. If your company is on the path to becoming a Bottle Rocket, it may look like Dell Inc.

Dell didn't start out as a Bottle Rocket. It began with an innovative proposition: to sell computers directly to the consumer, with no physical stores or middlemen of any kind. Focused on efficiency and a sleek supply chain, it devoted minimal resources to R&D, simply locking in exclusivity agreements with chipmaker Intel and overseas producers. The "Dell Way" was famously fast, and its model became something organizations around the world copied and revered. But further innovation on the Dell Way was discouraged: in 2003, Kevin Rollins, founder Michael Dell's handpicked successor, stated in no uncertain terms that unlike most technology companies, Dell is not an organization "'where people think they're a hero if they invent a new thing.'"[3] It was the Dell Way or the highway.

For years, Dell was the unchallanged market leader, but the success started to fizzle in 2006. Times had changed but Dell hadn't. The company's conviction that more and more consumers would turn to online and catalog-based buying models like Dell's as their comfort level with technology rose proved false. By 2006, phone and Web sales of PCs had fallen and retail store sales had risen.[4] Dell ignored the signs that computers were becoming toys, entertainment systems, and objets d'art that consumers would want to examine in person before buying.[5] And of course, for what order-by-mail business there was, Dell's efficiency and direct-to-customer option were no longer unique.

Meanwhile, the commoditized PCs that research-phobic Dell specialized in were losing their appeal to the average consumer. Once consumers became more comfortable with PCs, it turned out they were willing to pay a bit more for a version with innovative touches and sleek design—something they could test out in a store before they bought it—instead of just ordering the same grey box they used at work. Dell maintained an edge only in the slow-growing, price-focused business sector. And although it had once been a fine example of speed-driven success, the Dell Way began to work against the company. Dell wasn't able to adjust its course to find success in a changing environment. It had been moving so fast for so long, it had lost control of its direction.

Its treasured business model under attack, the company scrambled to maintain market share. Revenue continued to increase, but Dell experienced a 51 percent drop in profits in the second quarter of the 2006 fiscal year.[6] In response to the emergency, Dell began to concentrate on profit over everything else, and archrival Hewlett Packard surpassed it in market share in late 2006. Meanwhile, the focus on profit alone caused new problems for the company: even though the market for laptops grew 19 percent in the third quarter of 2006, Dell's laptop sales were up by only 6 percent.[7] The company was turning a profit, but it was also indisputably underperforming in its industry—which put investors on the warpath.

Of course, 2006 was also a year in which Dell faced a number of other obstacles, not all speed related. The company endured a threatened loss of its NASDAQ listing, a recall of four million laptops with faulty (Sony) batteries, and the beginning of an investigation by the SEC over accounting practices. Michael Dell was named one of 2006's worst leaders by *Business Week*, singled out for "Worst Reaction Time" due to his continued dedication to the Dell Way. And 2007 isn't looking any better for Dell than 2006. In the first quarter of 2007, Hewlett-Packard's U.S. sales moved up another 26 percent over 2006, while despite a healthy PC market, Dell's sales fell another 14 percent.

On top of the lack of agility signified by the company's unwillingness or inability to adapt to changes in the market and industry, Dell's problems exposed its lack of aerodynamics. It became obvious that Dell had a culture of bureaucracy, a relic of its fast, unexamined growth. Although Dell's initial claim to fame had been its lean, streamlined way of working, the company was now being held back by red tape. In early 2007, Michael Dell reclaimed the top spot at the company he founded, and shortly thereafter he sent an email to his employees addressing the overwhelming drag that was slowing the company: "'We . . . have a new enemy: bureaucracy, which costs us money and slows us down. We created it, we subjected our people to it and we have to fix it!'"[8]

In the same note, he pointed to yet another problem—the lack of clear direction, focus, and understanding of the company's best interests. "'Look across your organizations and . . . think about what is best for Dell, provide the clarity and focus of leadership that we need.'"[9] He said that in the future the company must have "'clear priorities and a focused strategy.'" Dell recognized that his company wasn't aligned behind a goal its investors, employees, and customers cared about, and that trying to rush ahead without a clear destination would be destructive.

To move Dell out of its slump, the founder promised to "'consider tweaking the sacred direct-sales model'"[10] and to change the company into one that is "'bold in thinking and swift in action.'"[11] He envisions a "Dell 2.0" rising from the ashes of the Dell way. Whether or not it can catch up to the Age of Speed remains to be seen.

Although Dell embraced and actively pursued speed, the company's ability to harness the power of speed fizzled. If it is to survive in the Age of Speed, it must become agile, aerodynamic, and aligned, the three traits that enable people and organizations to go faster and to use speed to their advantage—to become Jets.

Chapter Nineteen

JETS

*L*ike Bottle Rockets, Jets embrace speed and actively pursue it; unlike Bottle Rockets, Jets have outstanding records for reaching their destinations safe and intact. They can swerve around obstacles without moving further from their goals. They are aligned toward a clear destination, a purpose that propels them forward, to keep them on course.

Jets harness the power of speed, turning it to their advantage. They are agile—open to change and innovation and in constant pursuit of new opportunities. They're aerodynamic—free from the drag that slows down others' lives, work, and organizations. And they're aligned—in pursuit of a clear goal that is true to their strengths, passions, and environment, with all of their energy focused on that purpose. Like Balloons, Jets have found their calling, but because they embrace speed instead of rejecting it, they flourish in their environment and need place no limits on their growth. They move fast, but not just to keep up. Jets see speed as an ally, a power that propels them further toward their desires faster, a beneficent force that increases life, growth, energy, and the value of what they do. They let the speed of their environment work for them.

Consider Google—an organization that knows how to harness the power of speed. First, Google is undeniably agile. Even if it pours remarkable amounts of energy and resources into an initiative, the company doesn't hesitate to switch directions if its best efforts fall short. For instance, despite the fact that Google had every intention of dominating the market with its own speed and innovation when it launched Google Video, the company changed its strategy as soon as it saw an opportunity in renegade upstart YouTube. YouTube was faster—it won out over Google Video in large part because users could see their videos online right away, without the two- to four-day delay Google Video imposed.[1] The lure of speed pushed YouTube over the top in the fight for members and audience. But Google still won: without skipping a beat, it bought YouTube. Google was agile, open to change, and in constant pursuit of the fastest solution for its customers. With that agility, it used speed to dominate the online video market.

FAST FACT

In surveys about Web search engines, people say the more search results the better, but when Google tested a system that showed thirty results by default instead of the usual ten, the results per page took a half-second longer on average to display. And believe it or not, a half-second is just too long to wait. Users got frustrated and didn't conduct as many searches.[2] So Google decided to give the people what they really want: fewer immediate—but faster—results.

Google has proven that it's aerodynamic, too. Despite the company's reputation as an excellent place to work, its labyrinthine interviewing and selection process was at one time so grueling and glacial that candidates who had interviewed gave up on Google entirely and took other jobs. But with a keen appreciation for the value of reducing drag, Google recognized that its hiring process was a problem and began to streamline. The company identified the spots causing the slowdown and took action.[3] The average number of interviews dropped 17 percent (with further decreases on the way), and the company began considering a program to hire for some positions in just two interviews. Most important, the faster process included new, more accurate predictors of success aimed at reducing drag further down the line. Part of Google's new hiring policy is to seek out overqualified people considered likely to be promoted multiple times.[4]

Google's ability to harness the power of speed doesn't stop there. For a while, the company's expansion into far-ranging initiatives was leaving many investors and analysts wondering how everything fit together.[5] But in late 2006, it became evident that Google was aligned toward a clear, cohesive goal. As *Business Week* reported, they aimed "to become the vortex of all modern advertising."[6] Despite attempts by Yahoo! and Microsoft to compete, Google's powerful alignment sped it into the top spot. Google cofounder and president of technology Sergey Brin said that the company's goal is to offer a "'complete sales and marketing platform for all advertisers.'"[7] Researcher John Aiken summed up Google's remarkable results to date: "'When a company starts advertising, it tends to go one place, and that's Google.'"[8]

By being agile, aerodynamic, and aligned, Google has managed to make the Age of Speed work in its favor. Speed pushes it further and further ahead of the pack; Google not only embraces speed but also harnesses its power.

So if we don't want to resist speed, limiting our potential like Balloons or risking obsolescence like Zeppelins, and we don't want to explode like Bottle Rockets—if we want to be Jets—we must learn to harness the power of speed. We must learn how to go fast in ways that work for us, not against us.

The next four chapters explore precisely how to do that: *how* to speed up, and more important, how to do it in a way that enables you to reap the most benefits, to use speed to your advantage. The following pages offer a strategy for thriving in our more-faster-now world.

FAST FACT

Google understands that its users don't want products that provide layers and layers of data about the answers they're looking for—they just want answers, and fast. The company cut the file size of its Google Maps home page by 20 to 30 percent to slash the loading time.[9] Its search engine features were designed to give fast responses to the most likely questions. Search an equation, and Google Calculator gives you the answer; search an address, and Google Maps shows you where it is.

PART FIVE

AGILITY

Chapter Twenty

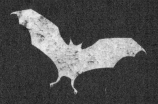

BATS

Ohio scientist John Zook made a remarkable discovery about bats. Studying the construction of their wings, Zook found tiny cells that resembled Merkel cells, a type of touch-sensing cell common in the skin of mammals. But unlike a normal Merkel cell, the bat cell had a tiny hair sticking out of it. To test whether or not the hairs affected bats' ability to fly and sense changes in their environment, Zook used the popular depilatory cream Nair to remove the hairs. Sure enough, when the bats had to make real-time adjustments to avoid obstacles or turn, they had problems. Said Zook: "'Sometimes they hit the ceiling.'"[1]

Bats' sonarlike echolocation ability and their elastic, membranous wings are most often credited for the speed and agility they exhibit when chasing prey, but Zook proved that they also feel delicate changes in air flow, which helps them adjust to shifts in lift, steer clear of obstacles, and avoid stalling in midair.[2] Behind bats' speed and agility is a mix of three primary traits: an uncanny ability to sense opportunity with their built-in sonar (in the case of bats, opportunity means prey, and bats catch their dinner before the insects even notice their presence), flexible wings that continuously change shape as they move (which helps them speed in and out of tight places to get food fast), and their ability to make adjustments and respond to even the subtlest changes in air flow (thanks to those tiny hairs on their wings—and the absence of Nair in bats' natural habitat).

FAST FACT

Almost one quarter of all mammal species are bats, which is cool . . . but also kind of disturbing.[3] And speaking of disturbing, did you know that unlike other varieties of bats, vampire bats can run? They use their wings as forelimbs and run like a four-legged animal—but their wings are longer and more powerful than their little legs, so they move less like a dog or horse and more like a tiny, creepy gorilla.[4]

In the Age of Speed, we can stand to learn a few things from bats: to be fast, we need to be agile—and to be agile, we need to cultivate the same qualities that our furry flying friends use to speed up. We need to develop batlike sonar to detect opportunities all around us. We need to be flexible (like their wings)—humble enough to identify weaknesses and brave enough to make changes. Like bats, we need to be sensitive to the changes around us, so we can make adjustments in response to those changes. If we don't, we may not fly into the ceiling, but there's a good chance we'll either crash face-first into the ground or never take flight in the first place. (BTW, the bats did recover from Zook's experiment. When their hairs grew back, their impressive aerial virtuosity was fully restored.[5])

Chapter Twenty-one

SENSING OPPORTUNITY

*T*hreats and opportunities for a business surface faster today than ever before. Globalization and technology have multiplied the ranks of potential competitors and customers—and raised the stakes of success and failure. This means that it's harder to compete and keep up with the rate of change, but it also means there are new opportunities at virtually every turn. To speed up when we feel we cannot possibly go any faster, we have to open our minds and our organizations to the world around us. We have to be more sensitive to new opportunities.

Take Proctor & Gamble, for example. It's hard to imagine a behemoth like P&G being fast and agile—the company has more than 135,000 employees in eighty countries supporting more than one hundred brands. But A. G. Lafley, CEO since

2000, is dedicated to making the organization more sensitive to opportunities outside its famously insular culture—and he's succeeding.[1] P&G is far from being a Jet, but the company is seeking ways to respond faster and faster to the ever-changing consumer vision of its commoditized products by looking for new ideas, new opportunities. P&G is trying to develop bat-like sonar.

Shortly after being tapped to lead P&G, Lafley made his first move to open the doors to new ideas for products. His predecessor had tried to cram as many products as possible through R&D, but the hit rate had dropped to about 20 percent. So Lafley de-emphasized the traditional role of R&D within the organization and set a goal of acquiring 50 percent of new product ideas from outside the company.[2] The whole point was to help P&G better connect with consumers' needs and desires and dramatically increase the speed with which the company got new products to market.

Lafley recognized a core truth: If you want to be faster, you need to be open to new ideas and opportunities. Before people and companies can flex or change, they have to welcome the notion that there's always room for improvement and be alert for opportunities to speed up.

As happens for many individuals and organizations, opportunity for P&G came from outside sources. In a market in Japan, for example, a P&G employee found a stain-removing sponge that really worked. He posted comments on the product on P&G's "eureka" catalog, an internal website designed to enhance collaboration. About two years later the Mr. Clean Magic Eraser hit the U.S. market, where it has since done well.[3] It took P&G half the usual time to get the product

If you want to be faster,
you need to be open to new
ideas and opportunities.

to market because it was able to partner with BASF, the German chemical company that owned the technology, to develop the product for U.S. consumers.

Then there's the garbage bags. P&G had developed a stretchable plastic for limited use with some of its own products, and Glad came calling. "'P&G had some interesting ideas it didn't know what to do with,'" according to Audy Baack, marketing manager for Glad. "'Glad had the marketing and category expertise to turn some of those into products.'"[4] Thus was born the ForceFlex garbage bag, which by August 2006 was number four in the market with $108.4 million in annual sales. In 2003, before the development of ForceFlex, P&G held a 10 percent stake in Glad. Six months later, after Force-Flex hit the market to much consumer applause, P&G upped its stake to 20 percent.[5]

Lafley has built an organization that is constantly on the lookout for new opportunities, and the benefits are obvious. Since 2000, P&G has introduced twice as many new products with elements developed by outside sources, and its stock price and its roster of billion-dollar brands have more than doubled as well.[6]

But it doesn't take the power of Proctor & Gamble to detect opportunities. Any person or organization with the ambition to be fast and agile can do it. You can do it, if you take the time to look outside your bubble—to get out of the minutiae of your life and work to identify opportunities that can get you closer to your destination without requiring more of your time. Do you spend too much time shopping for groceries? Turn on your batlike sonar and detect the unseen opportunities available to you. Maybe you could buy most of your packaged products from online retailers like Amazon .com, which sells everything from paper towels and cereal to shampoo and nose hair clippers (uh, at least that's what my friend tells me). And, hey, if it's an option, give your list to an assistant who can place the order from his desk and save you even more time. Go to the store in person only to shop for immediate needs and fresh foods. You'll spend less time in the store—and with fewer items, you may even get to use express self-checkout.

FAST FACT

In New York City, Fresh Direct, an online-only supermarket, delivers thirty thousand orders a week. They even have a "one-click recipe" function that allows a customer to choose from over four hundred recipes in its database, and the site automatically puts all the required ingredients into the customer's cart.[7]

Opportunities come in different shapes and sizes for different people and organizations, but one thing is true for all of us: if we seek more opportunities, we will find more opportunities. If we open our minds and apply dedicated, creative thought to how we can use all the opportunities available to us, we will speed up.

Chapter Twenty-two

BEING FLEXIBLE

To master the discipline of agility, we must also be flexible in our thoughts and actions—and this is an exercise in humility and courage. Being flexible is a test of our willingness to acknowledge weakness and take risks. After all, if we're perfect, we don't have to be open to change, right? And why would we need to take risks? Agility can be scary: trying new things can lead to new failures. Recall, however, the lesson we learned from Dell and consider how inflexibility can slow down, halt, or even roll back your progress. If we resist change, we forego the chance to speed up and achieve our goals faster. But if we're willing to recognize opportunities for improvement and risk failure (a possibility in almost any change), we'll be able to fast-forward through stubbornness, mediocrity, and slowdown.

FAST FACT

According to a recent survey, only 65.5 percent of CEOs, presidents, and COOs are open to criticism and evaluation, compared with 83 percent of nonmanagement workers and 78 percent of midlevel managers.[1] The most frightening thing about this analysis, of course, is that the more powerful you are, the more important it is to be agile.

Many people who are able to create lasting value in a short time share a common attribute: humility. These individuals have clear resolve and determination, but they also stay open to the idea that the way they're doing things may not necessarily be the best way—that a better way may be right around the corner. It's a vital part of being agile and a simple way to go faster in the Age of Speed. Think of the times in your life and work when you encountered the greatest resistance. Did you openly receive feedback that could've helped you, or did you stubbornly push forward with your agenda? In the end, what finally made the difference in your success or failure? If you're trying to speed up, you have to first open up.

But humility isn't a stand-alone solution. To be truly flexible or to create a truly flexible culture, we have to be willing to take risks—and we must have the courage to fail. Time and time again, stories surface about businesses that sabotage their success by playing it safe. Some companies spend so much time testing new products that they miss the chance to dominate a market; others stay cuddled in their safe zones while their competitors break new ground. Still others don't move forward at all.

To do things faster, we have to *do* things faster—we have to act, we have to jump. This requires a stomach for risk, because with change and progress comes a chance of failure. Nevertheless, no matter how solid their current situation seems, people and organizations that want to go forward faster have to explore new ideas and take risks.

The best way to identify the risks we need to take is to look at the risks we actively avoid, the risks that we're most afraid of. There's a chance that we're missing the big picture behind those particular risks, that we're blind to the opportunities they might present. Granted, some risks we avoid because they just aren't smart. (I avoid jumping out of airplanes without a parachute, for example. I might reach the ground faster, but those few moments I save before facing certain death don't seem worth it.) But there are other risks we steer clear of solely because they pull us out of our safety zones. Those are the risks we need to examine more closely: is it smart decision making, or just a lack of courage, that keeps us from going down those paths? Consider some of the risks you could take in your life that might help you reach your goals faster. What's keeping you from taking the leap?

Chapter Twenty-three

RESPONDING TO CHANGE

*B*eing open and flexible is crucial in our culture today, but if we want to speed up, we also need to be responsive—we need to adjust quickly and correctly to changes in our jobs, our economy, our family dynamics, our customer or colleague relationships, our worlds. On the surface this may seem elementary, but the issue runs deep in the Age of Speed. The rate of change has accelerated to such a degree that even people and organizations that *want* to be responsive are falling behind. Responding to change in modern times means being ultrasensitive to even the slightest shifts, rapidly analyzing those shifts, and taking appropriate action immediately.

Consider Pepsi, the number-two beverage maker in the world. Pepsi is faced with a subtle but profound change: its customers are becoming more health conscious. Sales of sugary sodas and other carbonated beverages are down domestically and slow abroad, and about half of all respondents to a recent poll said they were likely to consider nutritional value when selecting a beverage.[1]

Archrival Coca-Cola (with 80 percent of its sales dependent on soft drinks, compared with 20 percent for PepsiCo[2]) has promised relevant innovation but shown little. In the soft-drinks industry, the product-development cycle lasts years and the failure rate is high, so speed is vital.[3] Fortunately, Pepsi has answered the call with agility, openly and quickly responding to change. It has slated sixteen new products for release in 2007. The new products typify the healthier options consumers are looking for: teas, juices, energy drinks, and vitamin-enhanced waters are all represented, in multiple forms and flavors.

Each new product from the big beverage players is usually launched with an expensive and time-consuming marketing campaign. But Pepsi has found a low-cost option for trying out new ideas: placement in Whole Foods Markets. This trend-setting store's customers don't appreciate the huge marketing pushes typical of the industry: they prefer to discover brands and products free from the taint of mass marketing.[4] But sales at the stores not only prove how well the brand can do with a health-and-wellness market, they also influence other, more traditional stores to bet on the product. Pepsi's strategy has created a solid lead at least in the health-conscious portion of the market where it has endured decades of playing catch-up to Coca-Cola. Some may even say the tables have turned: "'We'll see how Coke follows up and whether they're too late if

Pepsi filled the holes in the market,'" says assistant professor of marketing Kenneth Herbst of the Mason School of Business, College of William and Mary.[5]

In the same way that Pepsi was sensitive to the subtle shift in consumer fancy and responded with quick action, we can all speed up by making adjustments based on changes in our environment. Consider it an agility imperative: a requirement for going faster in a world that keeps going faster. If we're agile and ready, we can respond and advance right alongside—perhaps even ahead of—our more-faster-now customers, competitors, and peers.

PART SIX

AERODYNAMICS

Chapter Twenty-four

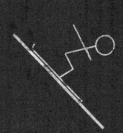

200

*I*n speed skiing, 200 is a magic number. At competitions, vendors sell T-shirts with "Life begins at 200" printed on them, and novice skiers fantasize about the number—all because at 200 kilometers per hour (125 miles per hour), skiers rocket into a speed warp: an unforgettable, mind-blowing, practically indescribable experience. The secret to getting there and staying there? Aerodynamics.

To go as fast as possible when speed skiing, you have to eliminate as many sources of drag or friction as possible. You wear a rubber suit that is so tight that, off the body, it looks like something made for a small child. You wrap duct tape around the ankle, where the boot meets the suit, to prevent even the slightest bit of material from catching wind. You shave down the edges of the small basket at the base of the ski pole to smooth it and cut drag while the poles are tucked under your arms, tight against your body. You wear a specialty helmet specifically designed to be aerodynamic (think Darth Vader's helmet, but tighter). You use long, wide skis to distribute your weight over a larger area and reduce the friction between ski and snow, and you wax your skis daily to further reduce that friction. Then, when you launch yourself off the starting line, you compress your body into a tight, smooth, bulletlike shape, squeezing your knees, elbows, arms, and hands together. All to reach the magic number.

If you hit 200 and can maintain your perfect aerodynamic form, you enter a sort of bubble, or pocket of space. You know that the snow beneath you and the trees around you are standing still and that you're the thing hurtling down the mountain at a breakneck pace, but it seems as though everything outside your speed bubble is in a state of utter chaos. Suddenly, you're shooting through a perfect, silent tunnel with no clutter, no distractions, no disorder. When you reach 200, you understand that aerodynamics creates not only greater speed, but also a smooth, euphoric ride.

The concept works the same way in business and everyday life. To be aerodynamic is to be free of clutter, to be in your metaphorical perfect form, ensuring that excessive drag doesn't slow you down and add chaos to your organization, work, family, relationships, and well-being. It may seem obvious that an aerodynamic, clutter-free approach to work and life would be an effective way to get ahead in the Age of Speed, but cutting drag isn't always straightforward. In fact, some kinds of clutter actually make you feel you're going faster, even as they slow you down.

FAST FACT

Drag is the mechanical force that opposes a body's motion through air or water—essentially, fluid friction.[1]

Chapter Twenty-five

Before

After

IT'S A DRAG

Today's most common source of drag for individuals is obsessive multitasking—ironically, something we do in an effort to speed up, to get more out of each moment. We crave immediate access to information and people, regardless of what else we're doing. We love to respond and be responded to quickly. We multitask to stave off boredom or because it seems the only way to get everything done. We use speakerphone to check voicemail so we can sort through email and snail mail while listening to other messages. We carry a Black-Berry to check email at any time and in any situation (no matter what else we might be doing). We don't even like to eat without doing something else at the same time: 91 percent of Americans watch television while they eat, 26 percent admit that they "often eat while driving," and 35 percent eat lunch at their desks while reading, working on the computer, or making and receiving phone calls.[1] We've become compulsive real-timers, answering calls, responding to emails, and pursuing data and people the moment they're available.

The problem is that multitasking doesn't necessarily speed us up; sometimes it slows us down. It adds clutter and chaos to our lives in an era that demands speed as never before. Brain-scan studies reveal that if we do two tasks at the same time, we have only half of our usual brainpower to devote to each.[2] So when we multitask—when we drive and talk on the phone or listen to a coworker while reading emails—we're really only half there for each activity. We cannot possibly give the full benefit of our attention or receive the full benefit of another person's input if we're splitting our focus, so we dilute our engagement and thus *increase* the time it will take to complete both tasks. How many times have you had to ask someone to repeat what she said because you were reading an email while she was talking? Did multitasking reduce the time you spent in the conversation or increase it?

Multitasking isn't the only issue. A different but related trend is that of accepting constant interruptions. A study involving thirty-six office workers found that, on average, they spent only eleven minutes of a typical workday focused on a given task before being interrupted—and once interrupted, it took them nearly a half-hour to return to the task, if they did so at all.[3] Another study of more than eleven thousand office workers revealed that interruptions caused more than two hours of lost productivity per day—25 percent of the workday wasted.[4] That lost time isn't cheap. Using an estimated hourly wage of twenty-one dollars for knowledge workers, the researchers concluded that workplace interruptions cost the U.S. economy nearly $600 billion annually.[5]

FAST FACT

Multitasking and gadget interruptions are being mentioned more often in therapy sessions. Family therapists report that children feel neglected and rejected when their parents obsessively check email during their time together.[6] And one Massachusetts psychiatrist told *Time* magazine of a patient whose husband insisted on keeping his BlackBerry in the bed while making love.[7]

But even if accepting interruptions has a negative effect on productivity, it would be foolish to suggest that we should—or could—stop it altogether. In the Age of Speed, the idea that we can proceed through our days by focusing on one project until completion, then another and another, is unrealistic, even a bit obtuse.

At the dawn of industrial capitalism, work was structured monochronically: we began a task and completed it before beginning another one.[8]

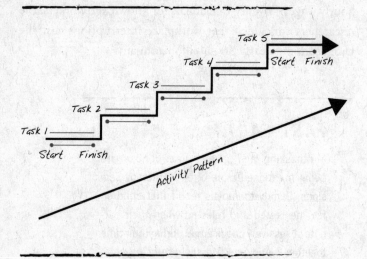

Our activity pattern was simple and linear, and our personal productivity was structured in neat, discrete segments—task 1, start to finish; task 2, start to finish; and so on.

Today, however, we face real-time demands, so the way we work is more complex. We begin one task, shift to another, start something else, complete the first thing we started, continue the third thing we started, and so forth.[9]

It's gotten to the point that our activity patterns aren't even linear any more. We can—and often must—respond to issues as they arise, so our activity shifts from task to task as we race to keep all our plates spinning. Now that we have the technology for it, it is expected that we will continually toggle between tasks, anytime and anywhere. It is no longer possible or practical to avoid multitasking or to ignore interruptions. If we try, we sacrifice the very tools that we've invented to meet the demands of a growing internal and external customer

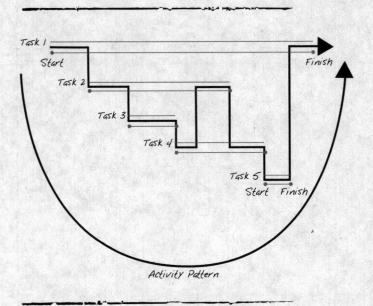

Activity Pattern

base—the tools that since the early '90s have vastly improved worker productivity.[10]

Obviously, multitasking isn't *all* bad. But if we're trying to do six things at once and dealing with constant interruptions, we lose focus and efficiency and have to work longer to get things done. So how do we balance the speed benefits that interruptions and multitasking can provide with the clear drag they exert?

Chapter Twenty-six

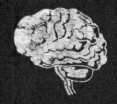

An Exercise in Consciousness

The answer to our multitasking dilemma is to take a conscious, analytical approach. We need to allow the disruptions that add speed, but avoid the ones that detract from it. A basic psychological premise states that some stimulation or arousal increases our productivity, but too much reduces it. Gloria Marks, a researcher at the University of California, relates the principle directly to multitasking: "'You would expect that a certain amount of multitasking would increase arousal, perhaps leading to greater efficiency. But too much will produce declining performance.'"[1] To simplify our lifestyles and cut back on unnecessary drag, we have to take control over what interruptions we accept and when we choose to accept them—when to multitask and when to focus.

Fifty-five percent of workers said they opened incoming email almost immediately, regardless of how busy they were.

The first step is to evaluate the importance of each task and decide whether to let it be interrupted. Is the interruption more important than the current task? Is it worth a half-hour's lost productivity? This may seem a no-brainer, but we don't always take the time to apply priorities to interruptions. In a recent survey, 55 percent of workers said they opened incoming email almost immediately, regardless of how busy they were.[2] But if we consciously assess the importance of the interruption and decide whether it's worth the switch, our behavior and results will more accurately reflect our priorities.

For decisions about multitasking, ask yourself whether it's best to stay fully engaged in the activity at hand. If your child is telling you about his day in school and you get a text message on your cell phone, you should probably resist the urge to check the message immediately; your child takes priority. But if you're working on a long-term project and a client emails you with an urgent question, your general productivity, work relationships, and well-being probably won't be compromised if you accept the interruption—in fact, they could suffer if you choose to ignore it. Being conscious of these distinctions helps us reap the benefits that come with being fully engaged in moments of significance—whether those moments are meetings with clients, conversations with friends, or experiences with family—without relinquishing the benefits of multitasking.

Next, we need to examine the total number of interruptions we allow and how often we multitask. Researchers at the University of Oregon found that our memories are compromised when we let constant interruptions distract us. The brain's memory and organization centers can be damaged when flooded by stress hormones—a common reaction to multitasking or interruptions.[3] By juggling too many tasks or allowing too many distractions, you condition your brain to stay overstimulated, weakening your ability to concentrate.[4] Not only is productivity (and therefore speed) compromised, but so is a valuable skill—being engaged when it can benefit you.

Finally, we need to assess what kinds of tasks we're trying to perform simultaneously. Multitasking is a good option only if what we're doing is unimportant or simple enough that the decreased brainpower (remember, it's cut in half when we do two things at once) won't negatively affect our productivity or results. To handle more than one complex task at a time, the brain, because of its inherent information processing limitations, simply must slow down. Otherwise, errors multiply and we end up taking twice as long, or longer, to complete each task.[5] One task dominates the other in terms of brain function and attention, so we're not really doing two things at once, we're just toggling between the two tasks—each interrupting the other.

In the workplace, excessive multitasking and unexamined interruptions hurt productivity. So what can organizations do to avoid slowdowns? Find ways to help employees take a step back and focus, when they need to, and devote time to the high-value work you want them to do. Some companies designate time each week, each month, or each quarter for work only: no meetings, no expectations for immediate response, no pop-ins. Dow Corning sets aside one meeting-free week each quarter. IBM reserves time on Fridays for employees to focus on work they might otherwise have to complete outside regular work hours.[6] If such time is to be used effectively, interruptions must be kept to a minimum. Doors should be closed, employees should refrain from checking email every five minutes (unless it's essential to the job), and nobody should be stopping by to share information that could be provided in an email or at another time.

Chapter Twenty-seven

TOO MUCH OF A GOOD THING

*O*nce we've rid our workdays of unnecessary interruptions and productivity-sapping multitasking, work becomes less cluttered—more aerodynamic and faster. But if there's still just too much to do, consider ways to filter and process the information and work that's pouring onto your desk.

The fact of the matter is that we all get sidetracked, distracted, and waylaid, and in the Age of Speed it's almost inevitable because of a profound shift in accessibility and constantly changing demands. Where once there were natural limits on how many people you could contact in a day and how much you could learn in an hour, now there's a fair chance that you contact more people and seek out more information—more data, more entertainment—each day than you did in a week

We drown ourselves in
trivia and excess.

ten years ago. But our receiving tactics haven't changed to compensate for the increase in volume. We still collect every scrap of data available and digest almost every email that hits our inbox. We drown ourselves in trivia and excess. We can spend most of the day tending to unimportant requests and soaking in expertise on any subject available. Does this make us more productive, or just busier? Does it make our lives better, or just more complicated?

Instead of simply letting this ocean of information and people flood unchecked into our minds, onto our desks, and into our lives, we have to limit the inflow by establishing trusted sources. This might mean signing up for email updates from two of your favorite online newspapers or industry news sources to keep up with current events—rather than consuming every piece of information coming to you. It could mean giving your direct line or cell number only to those you know well enough to be sure they won't abuse it—friends and family only, or clients you've known at least six months. It could mean protecting your email address using spam filters and other tools, so you receive fewer unwanted notes. Set aside time to review the volume of information, requests, personal contacts, and distractions that enter your life each hour. How much of that would you be better off without? There are more and more products and services popping up every day designed to help you filter through information, tasks, and decisions, so take advantage of them.

FAST FACT

When Apple committed to connect its iPhone to the AT&T network, the two companies revamped AT&T's voicemail system to let iPhone users filter their voicemail. Instead of having to trudge through all of their messages in chronological order, iPhone users can view a list of voicemails and select which, if any, to listen to.

Filters can help your organization, too. Competitive intelligence, for example. In most industries, knowing as much as possible about your competitors has long been a necessity, but gathering information was once a cumbersome, time-consuming process. It was difficult to determine what you needed to know and where to find it. In the Age of Speed, however, information is more readily available. Companies have websites and blogs that share information on their vision, mission, goals, and strategies. Employees (current and former) share information about companies in their personal blogs and through social networking sites like MySpace and Linked In. But nobody has time to sort through all of this potentially valuable information, so new ways are being devised to automate the process. Says QL2 Software's CEO and president, Chris Buckingham, "'Before, companies would be sitting on an island surrounded by scads of information; now they have some tools to help them sort through it.'"[1] QL2's own WebQL

3.0 is a pretty amazing tool. As it searches the Internet for information based on user-defined key words, it can assess the validity of the reference. For instance, it can determine by syntax and context that the term or phrase is being used sarcastically and bypass the reference.[2] With advanced information gathering and filtering tools like these, businesses can devote fewer resources to the process of making informed decisions quickly—a key component of being aerodynamic.

Chapter Twenty-eight

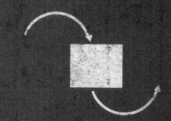

OFF THE DESK AND OUT OF THE INBOX

Once you've assigned priorities to each task and curtailed the amount of information that penetrates your consciousness, the next step is to process the tasks and information quickly. Note that this is not the same as completing tasks and consuming information. The difference is important. When you're completing tasks and consuming information, you're accepting them, doing any necessary work to understand or perform them, then following up to make sure there are no loose ends. When you're *processing* tasks and information, you may end up completing or consuming some, but others you pass on to trusted destinations.

A trusted destination is someone or something you can rely on to give you what you need without supervision. For example, if you get an email with a question you can't answer, you pass it on to someone who can—someone you trust to take care of it without your having to follow up. Unless you hear back from your trusted destination, you can assume it's taken care of *and forget all about it*. A trusted destination understands that a responsibility sent her way is hers, unless she lets the sender know otherwise. When a task comes her way, she takes care of it (or sends it to her own trusted destination) without further discussion.

Obviously, you have to choose your destinations wisely— and take care to hold up your end of the bargain—but the system at work is an aerodynamic wonder. There's no bureaucracy or anxiety involved, no time wasted passing the buck. You don't have to *do* everything on your to-do list—you just need to get it where it needs to go to get done.

If you're controlling input and passing tasks to trusted destinations but still can't process everything, you may be trying to do too much. Before concluding that you're overloaded, however, carefully examine every task you complete and all the information you consume. Is there really no one else who can do it *for* you, *better* than you? Delegation requires humility, a recognition that you're not the only competent person in your organization or family. When we take on too much and try to complete and consume everything rather than merely process it, not only are we being arrogant, but we're also slowing ourselves down and adding drag to our lives and work.

Within organizations, particularly large ones, determining trusted destinations can be difficult. The more bogged down employees get doing work that somebody else could do faster and better, the slower the organization runs and the longer it takes for individuals, teams, departments, and divisions to reach their goals. To help employees feel safe passing along tasks, contacts, or ideas to others, leaders and managers must foster a culture of trust and implement tools to make finding trusted destinations possible. In highly competitive environments, employees are less likely to trust their colleagues or consider them trusted destinations, so examining an organization's culture has to be the first step. Then simple adjustments to an organization's infrastructure can make fast processing and forwarding much easier—and more likely. For instance, an employee database that includes a list of key words for each employee can help others identify the specific work employees do, their knowledge bases, and particular skills and talents.

• • •

With multitasking and interruptions streamlined to increase speed instead of sapping it, your priorities in order, your filters established to help you take in what you need to know (and nothing else), and trusted destinations working seamlessly with you to process everything quickly, you can get the most out of the energy you invest in speeding up. The goal—for individuals and organizations—is to eliminate drag, to be sleek, to be aerodynamic. When we achieve an aerodynamic life or business, we've freed ourselves from the clutter, the detritus that can slow us down and keep us from focusing on our path and our environment. Once we are aerodynamic, we have the potential to be aligned.

PART SEVEN

ALIGNMENT

Chapter Twenty-nine

RACING ACROSS A TIGHTROPE

*I*n 1991, I raced across a tightrope—and not in the metaphorical sense. Back in the days when I was an Olympic speed skier, France had the best team in the world, so I went to Les Arc to train with them. In one of the exercises, the coach challenged us to walk from one end of a tightrope to the other as fast as we could without falling. As you might expect from a group of Olympic athletes, we were all very competitive, so we sized each other up, trying to guess who would be the fastest one across the rope.

One after another, each of us started across the tightrope, believing we could win. And one after another, each of us failed. No one won the race because no one could stay on the rope. We'd hold our arms out to our sides, keep our eyes on the rope, and carefully place one foot in front of the other. We'd concentrate all our energy on going fast and not falling—but then we'd fall. Again. And again.

Once we had accumulated enough bruising and humiliation, the coach let us in on the secret: to go fast, stop focusing on the rope, and start focusing on the destination. "Find a clear point of focus on the opposite end of the rope," he said, "and keep your eyes on that point."

One after another, we climbed to the starting point of the tightrope course and took a deep breath. We paused for a moment, and then looked up to find a focus point at the end of the course. We shifted our weight forward and started racing across the rope, never taking our eyes off the target. One after another, we got across the tightrope without falling—and with great speed. It worked like magic. Suddenly, the balance we thought we couldn't grasp was effortless, the footwork that seemed clumsy and impossible was natural, our frustrations were gone, and we could concentrate on speed. Once the target was clear and we stayed focused on it, the path and the process were simple—we were balanced and fast.

To thrive in the Age of Speed, we need to find our focus point at the end of the rope and never lose sight of it. That focus point is our authentic purpose, whether it be personal, professional, or organizational. When we are aligned with an authentic purpose, we can get from beginning to end of any course with ease, balance, and greater speed.

FAST FACT

Tightrope walking is also called funambulism
(not to be confused with fun *embolism*). The
Latin root is the combination of *funis* (rope)
and *ambulare* (to walk).

Chapter Thirty

AUTHENTIC PURPOSE

*B*eing aligned with your authentic purpose means that your goal, your focus point, is true to your deepest values and natural strengths and that your actions consistently promote that goal. When you pursue an authentic purpose and your actions are aligned with it, everything happens faster. Speed comes naturally, almost effortlessly, with fewer obstacles.

Philosophers since ancient times have pondered the nature of human and individual purpose. To help them define this elusive concept, they created words—*eudaimonia, teleology, orthogenesis*—and developed theories. Aristotle believed that the true purpose of all living things was to realize their inherent perfection. Maybe he was right; maybe our authentic purpose is the thing that lets us be exactly who we are—our authentic selves.

As I think of it, an authentic purpose is a goal that allows you to seamlessly integrate your true passion, true value, and true talents into your life, to use the elements of your inherent nature to your advantage. So identifying whether or not a purpose or goal is authentic requires an understanding, an awareness, of these aspects of yourself. But this isn't as daunting as it may seem. It doesn't require years of philosophical study or deep meditation—just honesty and analysis. To identify your true talents, look at the things in your life that have come easiest to you. To discover your true passion, think about those things that have brought you the greatest moments of fulfillment. And consider the biggest contributions you've made in others' lives or within organizations to understand your true value.

In some ways, it's easier to identify goals in your life that aren't authentic, because dissatisfaction doesn't hide well. Have you ever met a person who's frustrated because he has been chasing a dream for years and years and not getting much closer to it? Obstacles at every turn? Two steps forward, one step back? Perhaps he's chasing the wrong dream. If a goal is not authentic, not true to someone's real passion, speed tends to be elusive, and the destination may never be reached.

It's just as important for an organization to identify its authentic purpose as it is for an individual. If a business is trying to achieve something that its employees, leaders, investors, customers, or other stakeholders do not feel passionate about or at least connected to, advancement will come slowly, if at all. To find the authentic purpose, the leaders of an organization need to understand its true nature. What is its special value? What are its inherent strengths? What makes it a strong organization?

In the end, an authentic purpose is not just something people (individually or collectively) think they want—it's something they *feel* they want. It is that thing, that dream, that gives them a sort of emotional buzz—that thing they know beyond a shadow of a doubt is true and right. It's a purpose they believe in and a goal they can achieve because it capitalizes on their strengths.

But identifying the authentic purpose is only step one. All of your actions, both what you do and what you say, must be aligned with that vision if you are to achieve maximum speed. We face choices every day that can affect our authenticity, and if we aren't fully conscious, aren't vigilant in our efforts to maintain alignment, we can slip off course without even realizing it. For both individuals and organizations, it's vital to stay focused on the authentic purpose *and* make sure our actions consistently promote that vision. We hear sad stories of the opposite happening all the time: the retail company that lost sight of its authentic purpose after it grew too much or its founder left; the freelancer who can't speed ahead because she's doing work she doesn't feel passionate about; the marketing firm that gets nowhere fast because its clients and employees don't understand or feel connected to a purpose that matters to them; the technology start-up that has a great vision but gets distracted by seeking too many opportunities that are not aligned with that vision. Misalignment dissipates the energy of passion, but when people and organizations are aligned with an authentic purpose, they accomplish everything faster.

The focus required to identify an authentic vision and maintain alignment is well worth the effort, because when all of your behaviors and endeavors line up toward that vision, speed becomes simple. When you're aligned with your authentic purpose, you can make fast decisions and fast progress, because there is no battle with self-doubt, indecision, or confusion. Your path is clear, your focus is strong, your outcomes are evident. You attract the resources and energy necessary to move forward and avoid stalls that are unavoidable when the spirit behind an endeavor is inauthentic. Every decision, every action, propels you further toward your goal. Authentic alignment makes progress automatic—clear, smooth, and fast.

How do you find your own authentic vision and support it through your decisions, actions, and goals? You have to start with where you are and evaluate your current focus to see if it's locked onto a destination you sincerely want, need, and can get to. Are you hitting obstacle after obstacle in your quest? If so, it's worth it to question whether or not your target is authentic. Are you focused on not failing and all that requires? Are you focused on what you think you need to do? On what other people do? On what you want to do—what is true to you? Do you feel good about where you're going? Does it feel right? It's hard to define an authentic vision because it's unique to each person and organization and is affected by so many factors, but I will say that when you find it and set yourself on the path toward it, you'll know it, because you'll be moving faster than ever with ease and confidence.

Like so many things in the Age of Speed, achieving alignment requires profound awareness of the things you do in everyday life. Take a step back for a moment, examine the ways you're expending your energy and resources, and ask yourself, are they aligned with my vision?

Chapter Thirty-one

THE ALIGNED
ORGANIZATION

A businesses that is aligned knows exactly why it exists, is sensitive to how it fits into the world around it, and acts only in ways that promote both of those forces. It has developed a vision that is intrinsically suited to it, and it is focused on its destination, supporting its vision with every single decision, action, and goal. Because it knows exactly where it's going and is concentrating on getting there, it moves at top speed.

Nintendo is a good example. The specs for Nintendo's newest video game console, the Wii, came from an era long ago when things were (or seemed) simpler. Released at the end of 2006, the machine has no DVD drive, no internal hard drive, no high-definition capability. Its graphics are only slightly better than those of the last generation of consoles, released around 2000. And it costs only $250—compared with Sony's $600 PS3 and Microsoft's $400 Xbox 360.

But the lower-tech design isn't a mistake. Instead, it's a symbol of Nintendo's singular focus on gaming—its complete attention to providing the *experience* of playing a game rather than a system designed to be the nexus of all entertainment for a household.[1] Nintendo is aligned. It has an authentic vision and it moves closer to its vision with every action it takes. Because of that authentic alignment, Nintendo has moved into second place in industry market share.

While the competition is focusing almost exclusively on the market of hardcore gamers, Nintendo is going down a different path. Nintendo understands that graphics and technological advances—seen as vital to the hardcore gamers who traditionally make or break a system's success in the marketplace—are important, but secondary to the pursuit of its authentic purpose of creating a fun, engaging play experience for people of all ages and skill levels. Sensitive to changes in its environment, Nintendo is aligning its efforts with a growing market that its competition hasn't exploited. The company knows its purpose and doesn't waste time and energy on products or initiatives that don't contribute directly to fun games; it doesn't develop computers, televisions, or MP3 players. When an opportunity arises, Nintendo sees it first—and seizes it first.

FAST FACT

Nintendo has sold more than 2 billion video
games since 1985.[2]

In the design of its most recent offerings, Nintendo
played to its strengths and offered innovation in play instead
of innovation in presentation. The Wii has an unprecedented
motion-sensitive wireless controller that a user wields directly,
swinging it like a sword or a hammer, aiming it at the screen
like a gun, or twirling it above his head like a medieval sling-
shot—anything the game demands. Nintendo's DS portable
player, released in 2004, has a unique, innovative dual-screen,
touch-sensitive design. These advances have enabled Nintendo
to create games completely different from the competition's
offerings—games that appeal to a broad audience, not just
children and twentysomethings. Its DS game Nintendogs
involves raising and training digital puppies; the player can
actually "pet" these pets, using the touch-sensitive screen. Wii
Sports has gained a reputation for making players lose their
breath as they swing virtual racquets, bats, and bowling balls.
(Some players get so deeply involved in a game that they injure
themselves or the furniture—but that's another story.)

Nintendo's marketing is as aligned with its vision as its
product development: the company devoted 70 percent of
its launch marketing campaign to older and less experienced

gamers, people normally considered outside the gaming community. Nintendo earmarked $28 million to attract customers from a broad base of potential users.[3]

Seeking a broader audience for its games liberated Nintendo from a limited market of demanding full-time gamers and a console "arms race" with Sony and Microsoft—and opened the door to another possibility. Its remarkable alignment has helped make Nintendo the fastest-to-profit system developer. For Sony, each sale of its $600 PS3 actually means a $200-plus loss; Nintendo's $250 Wii sells for a profit. The costs of the entire Wii project were covered by January 2007 after a product launch in November 2006; Sony had to wait an estimated three years for a return on its machine.[4] Not coincidentally, Nintendo has made its core strength, its game software, highly profitable. Selling and licensing games is the moneymaking part of developing a console, and Nintendo sells many more games designed in-house than either of its competitors.[5] Games for the Wii often cost $10 less than Microsoft's or Sony's new console games, but Nintendo still comes out ahead in the battle for margins. Development for the Nintendo DS has a 70 percent profit margin; its costs are lower than those of its rivals.[6]

Nintendo increased its projected earnings for 2007 soon after the launch of the Wii proved that the newer system wouldn't cannibalize DS sales, and that the company was riding something of a wave. According to CEO Satoru Iwata, "'Demand typically shrinks after the Christmas season, but this year, we don't see demand slowing down.'"[7]

The success of Nintendo's approach shouldn't come as a surprise, though. Being aligned is like having a compass pointing true north. There's no question of which direction to head, what products to release, how to motivate employees and customers, or how to position yourself in the market. It's the definition of simplicity: the arrow points the way, and you follow the arrow. If you find an obstacle on your path, it's never hard to get back on track—north still stays north, your authentic purpose remains your authentic purpose. You simply find your way around the obstacle and keep north in your sights.

Chapter Thirty-two

THE ALIGNED INDIVIDUAL

*I*ndividuals who are aligned achieve their goals at a remarkable pace, because they pursue things that matter to them and make the most of their true talents. Consider Russell Simmons, the founder of Def Jam Records and CEO of Rush Communications. He is the quintessential entrepreneur, building businesses at a pace that seems superhuman to some—and most are successful. The list of enterprises in his entrepreneurial portfolio looks more like a jumble of disassociated organizations than a collection of well-thought-out endeavors designed to support a larger vision or set of talents. Look beneath the surface, though, and it becomes clear that Simmons has built an empire on two strengths. First is his belief in the commercial appeal of the culture and music of the urban youth of

America, both domestically and internationally.[1] Second is his unique talent for taking a business idea from inception to execution by pulling together the capital, the people, and the creative marketing to make it all happen. Each business, organization, or foundation he builds conveys a positive message of inclusion, acceptance, and progress for African American urban communities. Once he's built a successful enterprise, he moves on, selling it or handing it over to somebody else to manage. Simmons, a man of entrepreneurial passion, knows that wrangling the day-to-day details of any business is not his true calling. He aligns all of his endeavors with his true vision and natural talents—his authentic purpose.

Simmons learned the secret of alignment early, from the success of Run-DMC, the first band he produced—and the lesson has helped him stay true to his personal vision and goals. Run-DMC became a successful crossover band because it wasn't trying to be a crossover band. The group maintained their original, authentic New York–street style in the way they dressed and the music they created. This authenticity was the key to their success. "'You have to tell the truth,' said Simmons. 'It endears you to the community. The [people] can smell the truth, and they're a lot smarter than the people who put the records out.'"[2]

FAST FACT

Reverend Run of Run-DMC is Russell's little brother, Joey Simmons.

It's true that the businesses Simmons has developed vary dramatically in specific purpose—hip-hop record label Def Jam, clothing company Phat Fashions, entertainment ventures Def Comedy Jam and Def Poetry Jam, a hip-hop video-on-demand channel, urban marketing firm dRush, the urban youth political awareness nonprofit Hip-Hop Action Network, prepaid debit cards, a jewelry line, custom cell phones, an energy drink, and beyond. But each venture supports his authentic vision of an urban population that benefits from its own influence, and each is aligned with the market forces at play in his environment. When asked about his high-end, diamond-centric jewelry line, Simmons said, "'We in the hip-hop community have set the styles and created the trends that helped make many other brand names successful. . . . This venture will hopefully influence other African Americans to actively participate in businesses that they influence around the world.'"[3] His prepaid debit cards are meant to offer a solution to a demographic that often doesn't have access to bank accounts and other financial services.

Simmons has a vision that is authentic, and his behavior is consistently aligned with that vision. "'Stay in your lane,'" he says. "'If you're good enough, people will move to you.'"[4] Since his vision is true and he's making the most of his talents, he knows which projects and behaviors will benefit him. He doesn't waste time pursuing ideas that are not aligned with his purpose, and he doesn't have to spend hours or days making tough decisions. Because Simmons is an aligned individual, he steps forward quickly and with ease, all in pursuit of a clear, true vision.

Chapter Thirty-three

DESPERATELY SEEKING SIMPLICITY

*O*nce you have identified your authentic purpose and committed to aligning your efforts with it, finding the path of alignment is easy: to become aligned, seek simplicity. The principle of Occam's Razor is often interpreted thusly: All things being equal, the simplest solution tends to be the best one. But the foundation of this scientific assumption is a bit more complex than that. Occam's Razor is used by scientists to identify those theories that clearly contribute to the explanation of a phenomenon or the solution to a problem, to shave off the theories that don't actually contribute to the explanation, and to choose between competing theories by identifying the one that introduces the fewest assumptions into the solution. This limits the number of assumptions and theories relied upon and makes the final solution or explanation as simple as possible.

From this perspective, the principle of Occam's Razor can be applied to our search for speed. In our attempt to go faster, to *solve the problem* of speed, we must eliminate all of the tools, processes, technologies, ideas, business ventures, and other devices that are developed to speed things up but that aren't aligned with our authentic purpose. If we can isolate the things in our lives and organizations that are truly aligned with those forces, we will simplify our path and ultimately be faster.

This idea presents a curious and counterintuitive relationship between speed and simplicity. Simplicity is needed to achieve and maintain speed. So the act of pursuing speed in life and business results in an environment of simplicity. This is counterintuitive, because we tend to think of slow as simple and fast as chaotic; but fast can be the surest way to simplicity. Although we need simplicity to achieve speed, speed can lead to greater simplicity as we work to maintain our speed. By its very nature, fast is simple, so simplicity is one of the foundations of success in the Age of Speed.

Few businesses understand the principle of alignment—and how to use simplicity to achieve it—better than Royal Philips Electronics. The company is pursuing simplicity everywhere, all at once, all the time, in its efforts to recover from devastating losses in 2001 that forced it to lay off fifty-five thousand employees. What put the company in that situation? It was not aligned: its employees weren't working as a unit toward a common goal, and its infrastructure was anything but simple. "'Philips became so . . . compartmentalized that any time that a growth opportunity could be captured by regrouping resources, we missed it,'" said CEO Gerard Kleisterlee. "'The resources were in different silos and weren't accessible. That's what we've tried to change.'"[1]

But the devastation did help the company reach a critical point of understanding. If it couldn't eliminate internal barriers that kept it from being aligned and fast, it couldn't focus, couldn't capitalize on key strengths, couldn't compete, and couldn't survive. So Philips began the process of shaving off all divisions, products, and points of focus that weren't aligned with its authentic purpose. It was a long, arduous process. The company looked at each division, each product, each initiative to make sure all efforts were aligned.

Philips found its authentic purpose and transferred all of its energy to only those products and divisions that were aligned with it. At its core, Philips was an end-user electronics company, and that's what it had to act like if it wanted fast progress. By 2004, it had cut its thirty divisions down to five. In 2006, after many years of waffling, the company focused on health care electronics (e.g., medical imaging machines) and consumer electronics.[2] By the end of 2006, it had sold the majority share of Philips Semiconductor; sold 8.4 million shares of its stock in FEI Co., a manufacturer of electron microscopes; and picked up Intermagnetics General, a manufacturer of superconducting magnets used in Philips's MRI systems.

But the company's efforts to simplify may be most apparent in its North American consumer electronics division, which in 2004 hadn't turned a profit in fourteen years. The pressure was on; in 2001 Kleisterlee indicated that he would close the division if it didn't turn a profit in the next few years. Enter Reinier Jens. As CEO of the division, Jens reduced the number of products sold in the United States from six hundred to one hundred. He instructed sales reps to focus their efforts on only the one hundred largest retailers (75 percent of the business is with the ten largest), letting go of hundreds of smaller, unprofitable accounts.[3] These changes have helped speed up Philips's climb in North American market share: starting with only 5.4 percent of the LCD flat-panel television market in 2005, it reached 19.3 percent only one year later.[4] In 2006, Philips's North American division posted a small but triumphant profit of 0.5 percent net of sales.

FAST FACT

For Philips, simplicity wasn't just an idea for streamlining infrastructure or making products easier to use. It became a way of life, a new way of business, and a new way of thinking. In 2004, Philips established a simplicity advisory board composed of people from outside the company and from other industries who could help it identify ways to focus on simplicity in its products, marketing, and business practices. One member of the board was John Maeda, the author of *The Ten Rules of Simplicity*. In his book, Maeda recommends—among other things—subtracting the obvious and adding the meaningful (a take on Occam's Razor).

By identifying and eliminating everything that was not aligned with its authentic purpose, Philips eliminated the things that were slowing it down. Since by its very nature fast is simple, the fastest way for the company to reach its goals was to follow the simplest path. Simplicity is essential to—the foundation for—becoming aligned. It is nearly impossible to be complex and also be aligned and fast.

Navigating your life or the path of an organization when you're not aligned is like figuring out which way is north by looking at your shadow instead of using the compass in your hand—it's vagueness, doubt, and hesitancy versus precision, confidence, and speed. Being aware of the importance of alignment and conscious of its benefits in the Age of Speed will motivate us to discover our authentic vision and put all our efforts behind it. Without authentic alignment, we cannot achieve top speed; with it, we can accomplish phenomenal things.

PART EIGHT

HARNESSING THE POWER OF SPEED

Chapter Thirty-four

AIKIDO

When face-to-face with speed, we need to reach for it and turn it to our advantage—as a little Internet mail order business in northern California began to do in 1997. The company specialized in providing products its clients could get at brick-and-mortar stores around town, but with better prices, better selection, and better convenience (the customer didn't even have to leave home). It was fast, too: in its home town, customers' items generally showed up within twenty-four hours. The company had it all—price, selection, convenience, and speed—and its success in the local market set it up for expansion. Los Angeles was the obvious second market—a huge pool of potential customers not far from headquarters. But the city was out of range of the company's warehouses, so L.A. customers wouldn't get the quick delivery its local clients enjoyed. Suddenly, the company faced a decision: downplay the importance of speed to its customers, or reach for speed and turn it to its advantage.

Speed had served the business well so far—its speed of delivery was a known factor in its success. But embracing speed was risky. It would require building a new distribution center, and the company's profits wouldn't cover the cost. The company would have to borrow money—a lot of it. On the other hand, if the company resisted speed, it could avoid the risk of going heavily into debt to try its hand in a new market. After all, countless businesses have been successful on a lot less than cost savings, selection, and convenience. Fast delivery was just one of many benefits the company offered current customers. With proper marketing, customers in the late '90s might have been convinced that waiting two or three days to get what they ordered was a fair trade-off for the other benefits.

But the company's leaders thought differently. They figured that if they met and even exceeded the demand for speed, they'd put themselves in a sweet spot for growth and market domination. Competitors might be able to lower their prices, expand their selection, and even figure out a way to offer greater convenience, but if the company took the leap and used the power of speed to its advantage, how could anyone compete? Actively seeking speed would give the business momentum it could use to keep expanding. So the owners put it all on the line and decided to embrace speed. With a strong vision toward future growth, the company incurred $137 million in net losses in its first four years as it built a distribution system that could ensure fast delivery to every new area it served.

The investment paid off. The once-small California company Netflix became by 2006 a publicly traded corporation with 1,350 employees and $996.7 million in gross revenue.

Netflix can get DVDs to more than 90 percent of its customers in one business day, and its membership has increased from 239,000 in the first year to more than 6 million in 2006.[1] Despite the heavy investment in building the national distribution network, Netflix turned a profit of $14.9 million in 2006.[2]

FAST FACT

In January 2007, Netflix implemented a long-planned system to eliminate the transit time altogether by offering instant viewing of movies and TV shows.[3]

• • •

The difference between the way Netflix embraced—even pursued—speed and the way many people and organizations face it is like the difference between boxing and the martial art aikido. Boxing focuses on blocking or avoiding advances and attacking challengers with punches, or opposing force; aikido teaches us to reach for the opponent and use the power of the oncoming force to our advantage. In the Age of Speed, it's the solution for going faster—to reach for speed and turn it to our advantage.

FAST FACT

The founder of aikido, Morihei Ueshiba, was one of the fastest men of the twentieth century. Legend has it that he once managed to disarm an enemy who was twenty feet away in less time than it took his opponent to squeeze the trigger of a pistol.

It works like this: When we fight an oncoming force, as in boxing, we must block the advance of our opponent, avoid the opponent's advance altogether, or meet the energy of the oncoming force with a punch. We either succeed and avoid or overpower the opponent, or we fail and waste both the energy of our opponent and the energy of our own advance. Regardless of the outcome, there is usually an impact (probably painful), and both combatants are weaker after the clash.

In aikido, there is no impact, and the energy of one force feeds the power of the other. Imagine that an opponent is approaching you. Instead of feeling fear and resistance, standing rigidly on the defensive and ready to block the attack, you are relaxed, calm, and prepared. You anticipate the opponent's approach, reach for him and draw him near, then use the power of his energy and momentum to your own advantage by guiding him in the direction of your choice. No impact, no pain. Your energy and your opponent's combine to move you both in the same direction with more power than either of you could have produced alone.

Rather than trying to fight or avoid speed, Netflix adopted a more evolved approach. What founder Reed Hastings and his team knew was that if they tried to fight speed, spending money on a marketing program that played up the other benefits of their services, the demand for speed could prove to be too strong to defeat. They might spend all that money and still lose out to competitors if customers were irritated by the wait. Even if they succeeded, even if they convinced customers that the wait was worth access to all the other benefits, their position would be weaker without the power of speed behind them. Instead, they anticipated it, reached for it, and used its power to their advantage. Not only did they build a distribution network to deliver their products quickly around the country, but they also looked for less obvious ways to use speed to grow and strengthen their company. Seeking speed became part of their culture. For instance, to enable fast expansion and smooth entry into new markets, they developed a way to make a new distribution center fully functional within as little as forty-eight hours once they secure the real estate. They get the machines set up, hire the staff, and then bring an experienced manager in from another hub to get the operation up and running as fast as possible.

Anticipating the power of speed and actively seeking it gave Netflix, and can give us, the ability to become an agent of speed rather than a passive respondent to it. As the world continues to run faster, these principles will enable us to use speed to our advantage. Instead of wearing ourselves out trying to resist it, we can take matters into our own hands. We can leverage speed, using it to attain our goals. When we do that, we can get ahead of the rush, the demands, the exhaustion. Once and for all, we can make speed an ally.

Chapter Thirty-five

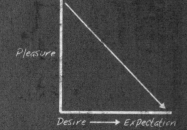

ANTICIPATING SPEED

Anticipating speed means actively preparing for the demands of our new environment—greeting speed on the front porch instead of hiding behind the curtains while it kicks down the door. We know speed is on the way (we're asking it to come), so we should prepare for it, discover how to put its energy to use.

If we don't learn to anticipate speed now, the consequences will become more and more negative over time, because the demand for it will only continue to increase. For more and more people every day, speed has become an expectation. If we find Internet access at a café or hotel, we *expect* it to be high-speed (and free). When we sign up for a new service, we *expect* to have automatic payment options to speed up the chore of

The difference between expectation and desire is subtle, but important.

paying bills. We *expect* to access information with a few clicks of the mouse. The desire for speed becomes the expectation of speed in more and more areas of our lives every day.

The difference between expectation and desire is subtle, but important—particularly in regard to the consequences we face when we anticipate or fail to anticipate each. When we anticipate a customer's desire, we leave her feeling pleased, maybe even impressed. When we anticipate an expectation, however, we merely affirm our competence (think about the "meets expectations" rating in a performance review). The customer isn't likely to be impressed, just satisfied. So is anticipating a desire more important than anticipating an expectation? Hardly. Imagine that you arrive at a restaurant, the maitre d' seats you, and your waiter immediately appears bearing water, a bowl of lemon wedges, a selection of hors d'oevres (not just bread and butter), and a drink menu. He waits for you to decide, then rushes off to fill your drink order. He has anticipated your desire for immediate access to food and beverage, for lemon with your water, and for something other than bread to snack on—and met that desire with fast, high-quality service. How do you feel? Probably impressed and pleased at his alacrity. Maybe you desired lemon for your water, but if the waiter had failed to anticipate your desire and you'd had to ask for a wedge, would you have been irritated? Probably not.

But what is the reaction when we fail to anticipate an expectation? Imagine that you arrive at a restaurant, are seated, and aren't given menus. You wait. Finally, a waiter brings menus and bread and butter. You realize you don't have silverware or water. Eventually, you ask a busboy to bring some, and maybe some napkins while he's at it. How do you feel now? You're probably irritated. You expect to receive a menu when you're seated. You expect to have silverware and a napkin before you have food. If we merely want something, such as lemons for our water, we're happy to have it, but not actively disappointed if we don't get it. But if we expect something, such as a menu, we are satisfied to have it and frustrated if we don't get it. If we fail to anticipate an expectation for speed, we face the judgment that comes with a poor first impression. We create a bad taste in the customer's mouth, and it will take some fancy footwork to change that feeling of irritation.

Our desire for speed has almost completely evolved into full-fledged expectation. We hate waiting in line, waiting for a website to load, waiting for service, and having to bumble through a long-winded automated phone menu. We endure it when necessary, but we get impatient and complain, sometimes even refusing to do business again with a company that has monumentally failed to meet our expectation for speed. As our expectation for speed is met more regularly and in more situations, that expectation spreads to more and more facets of life.

Speed is rapidly becoming a commodity, and if we fail to compete on the area of speed in our environments, our markets, we'll have no chance of attracting customers, clients, or investors. Anticipating speed is not only necessary in order to be wildly successful, but it's also necessary in order to survive in the business world.

The stakes are higher now. Like any trend, the expectation for speed must be anticipated if it is to work for us instead of against us. Anticipation is the first lesson we can learn from aikido, and it is the first way to become an active agent of speed. Once we anticipate speed and understand that the stakes are rising, the next step in an active approach to the advance of speed is to step forward and reach for it, to seek it out.

Chapter Thirty-six

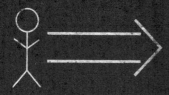

SEEKING SPEED

Most of us already seek speed in the most obvious sense: we look for shortcuts in our commutes, we streamline production lines, and we embrace faster and faster technology—at home and in the office. But to get ahead in the Age of Speed—to use speed to our advantage at a time when demands are turning into expectations—we need to seek speed in more innovative ways. We need to pursue not only the obvious avenues, where speed is a clear necessity, but also the unexpected ventures, where speed can lead to remarkable results.

My favorite restaurant in Austin, Texas, is a Japanese joint called Uchi. The food is always phenomenal and the service is great, but what really makes this place stand out is the energy in the restaurant. At the heart of this energy, of course, is speed.

I suspect that most restaurant owners, when considering how to seek speed, think about how to turn tables. The faster you serve the customers and clear the tables, the more people you can serve, and the more money you can make. But Uchi owner Tyson Cole saw an entirely different opportunity. He appreciated the value of speed and wanted to use it to his advantage, but he wanted his patrons to feel comfortable in his restaurant, not rushed. Eating at Uchi should be a unique form of entertainment, in Cole's vision, not just a place to grab dinner. He decided to use speed to get customers to come back again and again, not to get them to leave faster and faster.

Cole doesn't think the traditional appetizer-entrée-dessert model of food presentation fits in the Age of Speed, and he correctly anticipated that his diners would feel the same way. "Everyone has such a short attention span today. We don't want a plate to be sitting on the table in front of us for twenty minutes."[1] So Cole abandoned that model in favor of a series of small plates continually whisked in and out by servers. Diners have a new little dish in front of them all the time, keeping them engaged in the meal, and the servers quickly turning plates at every table creates exactly the kind of dynamic environment Cole was searching for. "It increases conversation. People have more to talk about. They're more engaged, and the experience is more entertaining." Cole uses speed to create variety, to create energy.

Tyson Cole reached for speed in a way that his competition didn't, and it sets him and Uchi apart—Cole was named on *Food & Wine Magazine*'s 2005 list of Best New Chefs in America. Because of the great food and certainly because of the dynamic atmosphere, Uchi doesn't have to battle the concerns that plague most restaurants in the same market. Because speed always creates energy at the restaurant, people don't reject the idea of going on a slow (read "boring") night like Monday—in fact, Uchi's Monday night business is as healthy as its weekend business. People are willing to pay for the Uchi experience, the Uchi environment, so packing in as many people as possible on Friday and Saturday nights is not a concern. Says Cole: "We don't have to worry about things like flipping tables fast."

Reaching for speed itself is straightforward; the complicated part is finding the right places and the right ways to apply a fast, innovative touch. Seeking speed is an exercise in consciousness. It involves constantly evaluating the task at hand, asking, "Can I make this faster? What would I achieve if I did?" Instead of performing routine tasks automatically, speed seekers use speed in unexpected ways to achieve unexpected results. They find shortcuts, increase efficiency, or streamline the system to maximize the value of every minute, but then they search for speed benefits beyond those boundaries. For speed seekers, boredom—their own or others'—is a warning that something's moving too slowly to keep people engaged, a sign of another opportunity to put speed to work. Like anticipating speed, seeking it out is becoming a necessity for success in the Age of Speed.

Applying the aikido method to your contact with speed— anticipating the oncoming force, reaching for it, and turning it to your advantage—is the ultimate solution for harnessing the power of speed. It is the antithesis of resistance and produces antithetical results. Where resistance results in conflict and diminished energy, aikido presents an opportunity to use the power of speed to your advantage. It's a shift in perspective and a change in behavior: rather than reacting to speed as something to combat or stop, you seek it out, constantly looking for new ways to use speed to your benefit.

Conclusion

*I*f we want to thrive in an accelerating world, we need to use the power of speed to our advantage. It's the only way to get ahead of the rush that seems to be overtaking our lives and businesses. My hope is that, having read this book, you'll have a new perspective, you'll feel empowered to take control of your time, of your tasks, of your priorities, of your talents, and start making your life everything that you want it to be and your business or career as successful as it can be.

Take a minute to think about the four profiles. It's true that the slower life Balloons lead sounds enticing, but few of us would be fulfilled with such a life, and few of us exist in environments that don't require speed on some level, and usually many. I don't know anybody who would actually want to be a Zeppelin or Bottle Rocket. So that leaves only Jets, and if we want to be Jets, we have to embrace a perspective that promotes speed.

To be a Jet is to appreciate the amazing benefits that speed offers—more life, more opportunities, and more significance. And it is to be conscious of how we spend our time, of the tasks we accept, of how we embrace speed or when we reject it. If we truly want to soar, we have to understand our authentic purpose, be nimble and open to opportunities, be free of clutter and drag that can limit our potential, and seek out speed in unique and innovative ways. These changes are key to thriving in our more-faster-now world. Your challenge is to embrace the oncoming force of speed and put these ideas to work in your life and business—to allow these concepts to inspire real action and extraordinary results.

Applications

SPEED AND YOU

Take a moment to consider how important speed is to you. How often do you prioritize speed over other variables? (Are you a Clear member?) Are there areas in your life in which speed should be a greater priority? Do you ever feel guilty for prioritizing speed?

What are the elements in your life that make you feel the greatest time crunch? Do the conflicts in demands on your time leave you with feelings of guilt or stress? How do you handle time crunch?

What is one area in your life in which you're afraid to speed up because you believe you'll have to sacrifice something else? Try to think of at least one way to speed up in this area or identify some minutiae that you could speed up in this area that wouldn't require a compromise of other values.

SPEED AND YOUR ORGANIZATION

Do you feel that your organization embraces speed as much as it should? Is speed considered to be a competitive advantage? What makes your organization fast or slow? What can you do to support the integration of speed?

What are some of the ways your organization actively resists speed? What is at the root of this resistance? What can you do to change the level of resistance or the perception of speed within your organization?

DEFINING YOUR PIE

In the Age of Speed, the lines are blurred between work, home, and leisure time. Track how you spend your time for a week and sketch it in a pie chart. Now spend some time thinking about your values and priorities. Draw up a list and determine how much of your time you think you should spend on each item. Sketch another pie chart. How closely are the two charts related? Use your values-based chart to help you make decisions when you feel conflicted about how to spend your time.

Create another pie chart for how you wish to spend your time, but this time focus on work priorities only. Show the chart to your manager to find out if he or she agrees with your analysis of your priorities. Now, how closely does the way you actually spend your time at work follow that chart? How can you speed up the things that seem to take up your time that shouldn't?

Is there a way to change the approach to work in your organization that would eliminate some of the time that people spend in meetings, answering email, or on general minutiae?

YOUR PROFILE AND YOUR ORGANIZATION'S PROFILE

Consider the four behavior profiles in the Age of Speed—Balloons, Zeppelins, Bottle Rockets, and Jets. Create a list of your attitudes and behaviors with regard to speed. Are they in line with one of the profiles? Are you a mix of the profiles? Are there behaviors that you can change that will bring you closer to being a Jet?

What profile is most fitting for your organization? Why? In what ways would your organization have to change to be more like a Jet?

BEING AGILE

In the Age of Speed, you must be agile. Rate yourself on the following attributes:

- Ability to detect opportunities in your environment
- Willingness to take risks for the sake of speed
- Responsiveness to changes in your environment

Think about something in your life or work that you would like to speed up. Take some time to consider opportunities that might exist for making that happen. Move beyond the obvious to the peripheral. Consider how something that seems totally unrelated might actually have an impact.

Take a few moments to consider some of the realistic risks you could take in your life or business that might help you reach a goal faster. Is avoiding the risk more important to you than achieving your goal faster or at all?

Consider a major change in your life or work in the past year. How did you respond to the change? Did it overwhelm you and halt your progress or did it surprise you and slow you down for a period of time? Were you able to quickly integrate the change into your life and make it work to your advantage? How would you respond differently in hindsight? How can you respond differently to change in the future?

BEING AERODYNAMIC

In the Age of Speed, you must be aerodynamic. Rate yourself on the following attributes:

- Effective multitasking
- Prioritizing and making smart decisions about how you're spending your time
- Identifying and utilizing trusted sources and trusted destinations

Become a conscious multitasker. First, look at your desktop at the busiest time of your day and make a note of how many programs and files you have open at one time. (Each web page counts as one, same for documents and emails.) Next, track your activities for one hour during a standard day. How many tasks do you start without finishing before starting, continuing, or finishing a different task? How are these activity patterns affecting your speed?

Make a list of everything that could or should be filtered out of your daily life and take action to do it. For one week, find a way to filter one thing out of your life each day. Unsubscribe to newsletters and publications you don't read. Ask colleagues and friends to avoid calling your cell phone unless it's important. At the end of the week, do you feel more free of clutter, free of drag?

Create a list of things that you regularly do that you believe are a waste of your time or that you aren't very good at doing. For each of the items on your list, is there someone who can do it better and faster than you to whom you could delegate such tasks?

What are the five things in your organization that create the most drag? Develop a possible solution for reducing each source of drag. Now do something about it! Send your thoughts or recommendations to the company leaders. Or, if you are a leader, take steps right away to reduce at least one source of drag.

BEING ALIGNED

In the Age of Speed, you must be authentically aligned. Rate yourself on the following attributes:

- Identification of an authentic purpose
- Pursuit of goals that reflect strengths, passions, and environment
- Ability to simplify in the face of complexity

Do you have an understanding of what your authentic purpose is? If not, do the following: Honestly assess your strengths, talents, and passions. Consider those activities and pursuits that give you the greatest fulfillment and the greatest emotional buzz. Now evaluate all of this information to help you formulate ideas about your authentic purpose.

If you understand what your authentic purpose is, do you feel that your short-term goals and your actions are aligned with it? If not, take steps to make it happen. What are some goals that you can eliminate or adjust to be more aligned with your true purpose? What passions do you need to bring to the forefront in your life to make your activities and decisions faster?

Can you articulate the vision for your organization with which your energy and time should be aligned? Do you feel like what you do is aligned with that vision? If you answered no to either question, why? Consider discussing this with your supervisor, posting a comment to your company's internal website or blog, or communicating about it in some other way.

HARNESSING THE POWER OF SPEED

Make a list of the top three things you'd like to spend less time doing. Then, brainstorm opportunities to go faster in those areas. Be creative, and list at least three solutions for each of the three tasks—even small solutions can make a difference.

Consider how the various benefits of speed could improve the quality of your life and work. Take a point of dissatisfaction in your life and list ways that speed could lessen that dissatisfaction or eliminate it altogether.

For more information on training, speaking, and consulting so that you and your organization can harness speed, check out www.vinceposcente.com.

Tips and Tricks from
the Age of Speed

The Age of Speed is about understanding the choices you make in the time you have. To eliminate the feeling of being overwhelmed or to thrive in a fast-paced world that demands more, you must first identify all the things that are important to you.

The tips below will help you identify your own personal set of values and experiences that give you joy. Consider words like connection, challenge, contribution, intimacy, learning, integrity, service, love, leadership, peace, excitement, variety, and problem solving. Are you spending your time in ways that reflect your values?

Then, think about ways to cut time where you can and gain time where time matters most. Throw out old ideas about the divide between work, home, and leisure time, and identify ways to put your passions into everything you do. Finally, think about how interruptions and multitasking affect your work and life, and learn how to control and prioritize your time.

IDENTIFY YOUR VALUES AND KEY EXPERIENCES

- **Spend Extra Time on Significant Experiences**—Make sure you spend your extra time on rewarding experiences. Frequently, when we reduce the time it takes to do something insignificant, we end up using the saved time on yet another insignificant activity. Use the time saved to reward yourself.

Example: One of Michelle's values and key experiences is connection. When she saves herself an hour by grocery shopping online she rewards herself with a phone call to a friend or to a business contact she hasn't been making time for.

- **Be Conscious of Bonus Time**—If you figure out a way to save time at the bank and the grocery store, for example, do you earmark that time for something rewarding, or do you just fill that time with other passive activities that pop up?

Example: Spencer uses the self-checkout kiosk at the grocery store and saves himself from standing in line for ten minutes. He then takes a moment to think how he will fill that extra time. Spencer decides to handwrite a thank-you note to a neighbor who stored his mail and newspapers while he was away the month before.

- **Use Speed for More Passionate Pursuits**—The key to using speed effectively is identifying the difference between repetitive chores and passionate pursuits. If you do something you love, that you have a passion for—paint, play music, study high-level mathematics—you may want to immerse yourself in the full experience each and every time. But you should use every trick you can find to speed up the things you don't feel passionate about, like cleaning the windows or running errands.

Example: Pria makes a game of looking for ways to make any process more efficient. The game has one goal: Use time wisely. How can I save time, no matter how small? In the kitchen she learned the preset buttons on the microwave and saves a few seconds each time she needs to heat something up. In the cutlery drawer she reserved four slots to hold a table setting. When it's time to set the table she saves a few more seconds. On the fridge she posted a list of groceries that she typically purchases. When she is close to running out she puts a check mark beside the item. This saves her a few minutes of having to take stock before dashing off to the store. Pria also used to do the dishes while she sat her kids in front of the boob tube. Now, she fills the sink full of hot water, soaks the dishes and does them after she puts the kids to bed. While the dishes soak she plays games with her kids and reads them books. It makes her feel good because she has more quality time with her children—and she saves water by not rinsing each dish for the dishwasher and saves scrub time on the pots.

- **Identify Value Relative to Speeding Up**—When choosing the best opportunities for speeding up, consider the value of both the experience leading up to the end (e.g., standing in line) and of the end itself (e.g., buying paper towels or concert tickets). When the value of each is small, it is a good opportunity to use speed. On the other hand, when the value of one or both is significant, speed may compromise the pleasure you get from the experience. You don't always have to go fast. The Age of Speed is about looking for the best use of our time to maximize the experience of life.

Example: Hanna has to deliver a package across town. The best use of her time might be hiring a courier. But today Hanna is picking up her teenage son from band practice, and his favorite pizza place is near her package's destination. The extra time it takes her to deliver the package herself buys her extra "talk" time in the car with her child and the opportunity for dinner with him, even if a courier might have accomplished the delivery more quickly.

REMODEL YOUR TIME

- **Rethink Work-Home-Leisure**—If we create a new alternative to the outdated work-home-leisure model, we will be able to take advantage of all of the opportunities available to us, and establish an individual purpose for using the time we save on the things that matter most to us.

Example: Pat takes her boss out for lunch to discuss how she can get better results from work. She admits that she resents getting emails on her BlackBerry at eleven at night, while at the same time she's frustrated that she's unable to take her child to the dentist at eleven during the day. They decide to test out a version of Best Buy's ROWE program, where employees have no set hours, for the next thirty days. By the end of the lunch, Pat and her boss target three key results for the month and decide to reconvene at the end to evaluate the effectiveness of their idea.

- **Blur Personal and Work Time with Passion**—Don't get fixated on ways to keep work out of your personal time— look for ways to put personal time and passion into your work.

Example: Victor takes an hour on Sunday night to review a list of things he is passionate about. He then lists the results that he wants to accomplish personally and professionally. Victor draws lines between the lists to connect his passions with his objectives for the coming week.

- **Evaluate then Improve Time Use**—It's no longer about how many hours you spend in the office; it's all about productivity and outcomes. This leads to a totally different evaluation of how you spend your time. Think about what you're doing and ask yourself, Is this going to help me reach my desired outcome?

Example: Nathalie lists all the outcomes she is expected to accomplish at work. She then lists all the activities she does on a daily basis. Beside each activity, she puts an H, M, or L (for high, medium, or low impact on the outcome). Nathalie might double-check her prioritizing with her manager then commits to doing the high impact activities first, the medium impact activities next, and then decide whether the low impact activities are necessary at all.

- **Don't be Afraid of Shortcuts**—If taking a shortcut enables us to be more focused on the aspects of a project that require our utmost attention, then it can improve the quality of the end result.

Example: Dexter has to prepare an RFP (request for proposal). He uses a RFP template to ensure that he doesn't leave out anything important. He Googles key words related to the proposal. Instead of making telephone research calls to stakeholders in the RFP he casts a net through email, looking for specific answers to questions. Dexter looks to save time in the development process to focus on the areas that need attention.

- **Lose The Guilt**—If we stop judging our time according to outdated definitions of work, home, and leisure, we are less likely to feel stressed out about the blurred lines, and we won't suffer when the areas merge—instead, we'll find solutions to our conflicts.

Example: Mia hires a consultant proficient in organizational manage-ment. Productivity is down at her company and she wants to know why. The report reveals that employees are feeling guilty about working at home on weeknights and weekends and feeling guilty about handling personal issues at work. Mia understands the importance of redefining the balance between work, home, and leisure. The importance of productivity: Produc-tivity goes up, turnover costs go down, and employee satisfaction improves with a solution that targets results in the organization. Mia formed a BEL (Balanced Easier Lives) committee that was charged with coming up with ways the company could help employees have more work-home-leisure bal-ance. BEL came up with a stipend to ensure all employees can have high speed internet at home. BEL also instituted activities that were permitted at work, such as vacation planning and in-house yoga classes.

BE CREATIVE AND FLEXIBLE

- **Find Time for Your Values**—Shift your perspective of time from a focus on tasks and physical location to a focus on values. Ask yourself, How can I explore the things I find meaningful while at work?

Example: Sophia changed her lunch routine once per week. She takes a bagged lunch to a local park, switches off her cell phone, and opens up a notepad. She lists all the things that give her joy and energy at work, and attaches values to those words. Things like solving problems, making processes more efficient, and connecting with suppliers relate to what she finds meaningful at work. Sophia finds this exercise gives her energy, keeps her focused, and saves her from wasting time.

- **Flexible + Humble + Brave = Less Drag**—Don't hesitate to switch directions if your best efforts fall short. We need to be flexible, humble enough to identify weaknesses, and brave enough to make changes. Responding to change in modern times means being ultra-sensitive to even the slightest shifts, rapidly analyzing those shifts, and taking appropriate action immediately.

Example: Ernie Lewis's father always told him that a Lewis never quits. But this advice had put Ernie in a bind more than once. Ernie made a new decision about how to respond in the Age of Speed. He would be flexible by reminding himself of the end result. If a sudden obstacle appeared in Ernie's path, he would look at it as an opportunity to find a different path that would still take him to his destination, like the pioneers who headed west. More than once, Ernie saw people slow down or fail due to ego or an irrational desire to be right all the time. Ernie put his formula to the test when he said yes to a volunteer position on a CPA association board. His hope was the position would benefit his career and give back at the same time. What resulted was too much time away from his family. His wife was more stressed and their kids were at an age where they needed their dad around. Ernie admitted his mistake to the board, promised to volunteer again when his kids were grown, and relinquished his position to a colleague in his office. He began coaching his daughter's soccer team and was able to spend more time with his family. He also made a valuable business connection with another coach who was also a CPA.

- **Reduce Minutia for More Time**—Take the time to look outside your personal bubble. Get out of the minutiae of your life and work to identify opportunities that can get you closer to your destination without requiring more of your time.

Example: Ken is a stay-at-home dad who wanted to find more time for the things that were important in his life. He found a local laundromat that would wash, dry, and fold his family's laundry for $40 a week. For Ken, trading a little bit of money for more time was worth it. He used the extra time to play hockey again at the local rink on Wednesdays and Fridays.

- **Speed Up by Opening Up**—Be open to receiving feedback, and don't stubbornly push forward with your agenda. If you're trying to speed up, you first have to open up.

Example: At every staff meeting Christa ensured that Process Improvement was on the agenda. Every two weeks she would pick a common task or even a long-standing routine that could be changed or simplified to save time. One of Christa's staff members approached her with an idea: to eliminate the letter of intention that the company wrote and delivered while contracts were being prepared. Even though the letter of intention had initially been Christa's idea, she saw the value of her staff member's suggestion. The next month they eliminated the letter and went straight to contract on bookings. The idea saved two weeks on contracts and eliminated the problem of clients backing out of intended deals.

INTERRUPTIONS AND MULTITASKING—THE TWO DEADLY SINS OF TIME MANAGEMENT

- **Identify Interruptions**—We have to take control over what interruptions we accept and when we choose to accept them—when to multitask and when to focus.

Example: Andrea was looking for ways to improve efficiency in the office. She found out that 55 percent of workers said they opened incoming email almost immediately, regardless of how busy they were. Andrea also remembered that the average time between beginning a task and being interrupted is only eleven minutes. Moreover, the average time it took a worker to get back on task was thirty minutes, if they got back on task at all. Andrea decides to make a game out of it with her staff and calls it The War on Interruptions. Each day for three weeks Andrea gives "tactical measures" or tips to combat the "evil empire" of interruptions, and after twenty-one days the workers get together and share their tips, ideas, and successes.

- **Eliminate Interruptions During Important Tasks**—The first step is to evaluate the importance of each task and decide whether to let it be interrupted.

Example: Mike is on the phone discussing an important process that needs to be implemented in his division. As Mike is talking, he sees a new email pop up from his son's teacher. It is titled, "We should talk." Mike opens the email while the phone conversation continues. While lost in the content of the email, Mike hears the words, "So what do you think?" Mike pauses, stammers and the voice comes back, "Are you reading email?" Mike lies and says, "No," but can't recover. From then on, Mike decides to eliminate interruptions during important tasks. He decides that each important task will have laser focus. During all phone conversations he hides the email screen. During email work, he switches his phone to Do Not Disturb.

- **Protect Your Priorities**—If we consciously assess the importance of the interruption and decide whether it's worth the switch, our behavior and results will more accurately reflect our priorities.

Example: Casey is having dinner with her husband and kids. Her Black-Berry beeps. The rule at the table is when it is family time, phone and email interruptions are not allowed. She lets it beep and continues on with her current highest priority, which is family time.

- **Separate Simple from Significant**—It's important to assess what kinds of tasks we're trying to perform simultaneously. Multitasking is a good option only if what we're doing is unimportant or simple enough that the decreased amount of brainpower won't negatively affect our productivity or results.

Example: Eric puts tasks into one of two buckets: Simple or Significant. With the Significant activities, he uses laser focus with zero interruptions. With the Simple tasks he layers a couple at a time. Today he grabs a stack of folders he has been putting off filing. At the same time he begins the hobbling experience of downloading a software program that has been waiting for his attention. With his spare time he even makes a couple of routine phone calls to book a haircut and get some change-of-address forms.

- **Budget Solitary Confinement at Work**—Designate a time each day, each week, or each month to focus on work that ensures you're the master of your time.

Example: During a designated time each week, Eric keeps his door closed for thirty minutes to an hour. He doesn't check his email every five minutes. He doesn't get involved in any conversations that could take place at another time. Eric uses this time to plan and prepare. His objective is keep from redoing work in the future. His "open door policy" is suspended during this time so that he can be future-focused. He knows that at speed there is time only to act. His long-term planning in "solitary confinement" saves him time.

- **Establish Trusted Sources**—Limit the ocean of information that reaches you every day by establishing trusted sources. This might mean signing up for email updates from two of your favorite online newspapers or industry news sources to keep up with current events.

Example: Steven decides that he will trim all things that create drag, and define specific trusted sources. Over the course of the next month he unsubscribes from all of the newsletters and updates that he ends up deleting every week. He only keeps a couple of emails that he typically reads. In addition, he identifies which people usually send him only trivial information and jokes, and files their emails in a 'junk senders' folder on his Outlook for when he has more leisure time.

- **Sort Tasks Instead of Immediately Accepting Them**—You may end up completing some, but others you can pass on to "trusted destinations." A trusted destination understands that a responsibility sent her way is hers to do unless she lets the sender know otherwise.

Example: Spencer sits down with his assistant and they decide that if he cc's her on an email, it is an automatic expectation that she is to act on it. This eliminates any secondary or follow-up emails that could cause drag.

Notes

Chapter 1

1 Jane Black, "Toward a Biometrics Bill of Rights," *Business Week Online*, November 7, 2002, www.businessweek.com/technology/content/nov2002/tc2002117_8617.htm.

2 Joe Buney, "A Business Boom in Seeking Safety," *CQ Weekly Online*, October 23, 2006, http://public.cq.com/public/homelandindex.html.

3 "Fly Through Security," *Kiplinger's Personal Finance*, June 2006, 20.

4 Ibid.

5 Verified Identity Pass, "Clear Facts," available at www.verifiedidpass.com/Clear%20Fact%20Sheet.pdf (accessed February 13, 2007).

6 "Biometrics Gets Down to Business," *Economist*, December 2, 2006, 21–22.

7 "Statistically Speaking," *Computing Canada*, June 17, 2005, 5.

Chapter 2

1 Aerion Supersonic Business Jet Specifications, available at www.aerioncorp.com/txt/press-kit/AerionSpecs20061016.doc (accessed February 13, 2007).

2 Jessica S. Vascellaro, "Seeing if Same-Day Delivery Works," *Wall Street Journal*, December 22, 2005.

3 Public Opinion Online, "When you are waiting in line in a store or office, how long are you usually able to wait before you lose your patience?" Sponsored by Associated Press/Ipsos-Public Affairs, May 28, 2006.

4 Laura Petrecca, "Stores, Banks Go Speedy to Win Harried Customers," *USA Today*, December 1, 2006.

5 Mya Frazier, "Progressive, Geico Prod Auto Rivals into Price War," *Advertising Age*, February 28, 2005.

6 Theresa Howard, "Presidential Allstate Ads Counter the Gecko," *USA Today*, August 16, 2004.

Chapter 3

1 Professor Daniel Hamermesh (Edward Everett Hale Centennial Professor in Economics, University of Texas at Austin), in discussion with the editor, December 2006.

2 "Finding Time," *Yankelovich Monitor*, November 16, 2006.

Chapter 9

1 Tara Parker-Pope, "This is Your Brain at the Mall: Why Shopping Makes You Feel So Good," *Wall Street Journal*, December 6, 2005, D1.

2 Claudia Wallis, Sonja Steptoe, Wendy Cole, "Help! I've Lost My Focus," *Time*, January 16, 2006, 72–79.

Chapter 11

1 Who Moved My Cheese? "Who Moved My Cheese: The Phenomenon," www.whomovedmycheese.com/whomovedmycheese/phenomenon.php (accessed April 12, 2007).

2 Michael Gartenberg, "Technology Now Defines the Business," *Computerworld*, June 31, 2006, 19.

3 Carol Kaufman-Scarborough and Jay D. Lindquist, "Understanding the Experience of Time Scarcity: Linking Consumer Time-Personality and Marketplace Behavior," *Time & Society* 12 (2003): 349–370.

Chapter 12

1 Bizarre, Almost Useless and Interesting Facts about our World, available at "Bizarre Fact #15," www.ebizarre.com/Category/Surveys_and_Statistics/2/ (accessed Februrary 21, 2007).

2 Martin Roberts, "'BlackBerry Thumb' Sparks New Form of Hand Massage," *Reuters*, November 10, 2006.

3 Carol Kaufman-Scarborough and Jay D. Lindquist, "Understanding the Experience of Time Scarcity: Linking Consumer Time-Personality and Marketplace Behavior," *Time & Society* 12 (2003): 349–370.

CHAPTER 13

1 Oliver Ryan, "Blogger in Chief," *Fortune*, November 13, 2006, 51.

2 Patrick J. Kiger, "Flexibility to the Fullest," *Workforce Management*, September 25, 2006.

3 Ibid.

4 Ibid.

5 Ibid.

CHAPTER 16

1 Spartacus Educational, "Zeppelin Raids," www.spartacus.schoolnet.co.uk/FWWzeppelin-raids.htm (accessed April 12, 2007).

2 About.com, "The Hindenburg Disaster," americanhistory.about.com/od/hindenburg/a/hindenburg.htm (accessed April 12, 2007).

3 Steve Hamm and William C. Symonds, "Mistakes Made on the Road to Innovation," *BusinessWeek*, November 27, 2006, 26–31.

4 Ibid.

5 Ibid.

6 Claudia H. Deutsch, "Kodak Posts Another Loss On Its Way to Going Digital," *New York Times*, November 1, 2006, C3.

7 Steve Hamm and William C. Symonds, "Mistakes Made on the Road to Innovation," *BusinessWeek*, November 27, 2006, 26–31.

8 Ibid.

CHAPTER 17

1 ThinkQuest Library, "Chinese Globe Lanterns," Available at library.advanced.org/23062/balloon.html (accessed April 16, 2007).

2 Leonard Zinn (owner of Zinn Cycles), in discussion with the editor, December 2006.

CHAPTER 18

1 American Council on Science and Health, "Protect Your Eyes on July Fourth," Available at www.acsh.org/printVersion/hfaf_printNews.asp?newsID=577 (accessed April 16, 2007).

2 Ibid.

3 Andrew Park, "What You Don't Know About Dell," *BusinessWeek*, November 3, 2003.

4 Louise Lee, "It's Dell vs. the Dell Way," *BusinessWeek*, February 23, 2006.

5 "Return to Founder," *Economist*, February 3, 2006.

6 Christopher Lawton, "Dell Loses Lead, and Investors Can Take Heart," *Wall Street Journal*, November 10, 2006, C1.

7 Damon Darlin, "At Dell, Profit Rises, Questions Linger," *New York Times*, November 22, 2006, C1, C8.

8 "Excerpts from Michael Dell's E-mail to Employees Friday," *Austin American Statesman*, February 4, 2007.

9 Ibid.

10 "Return to Founder," *Economist*, February 3, 2006.

11 "Excerpts from Michael Dell's E-mail to Employees Friday," *Austin American Statesman*, February 4, 2007.

CHAPTER 19

1 Elinor Mills, "Google Says Speed is King," *CNET News.com*, November 9, 2006, http://news.com.com/2100-1032_3-6134247.html.

2 Ibid.

3 Kevin J. Delaney, "Google Adjusts Its Hiring Process as Needs Grow," *Wall Street Journal*, October 23, 2006.

4 Ibid.

5 Susan J. Berfield, "Best (and Worst) Leaders of 2006: The Best Juggernaut, Eric Schmidt," *Business Week*, December 18, 2006, 60.

6 Ibid.

7 Robert Hoff, "Google's Brand New Appeal," *Business Week*, February 1, 2007.

8 Ibid.

9 Elinor Mills, "Google Says Speed is King," *CNET News.com*, November 9, 2006.

CHAPTER 20

1 Greg Miller, "Flying by Feel," *Science Now*, November 14, 2005, 2–3.

2 Ibid.

3 *American Museum of Natural History*, s.v. "Bats: Flap Your Hands" (by Adam Summers), biomechanics.bio.uci.edu/_html/nh_biomech/bats/bats.htm (Accessed March 9, 2007).

4 Cornell University, "Unlike Other Bats, Vampire Bats Keep Out of Trouble by Running, Cornell Researchers Find," Available at www.news.cornell.edu/stories/March05/Riskin.bats.snd.html (Accessed March 9, 2007).

5 Greg Miller, "Flying by Feel," *Science Now*, November 14, 2005, 2–3.

CHAPTER 21

1 Alex Markels, "Turning the Tide at P&G," *U.S. News & World Report*, October 30, 2006, 69–71.

2 Ibid.

3 Ibid.

4 Constantine Von Hoffmann, "Masters of Funky Flex," *Brandweek*, September 25, 2006, 23–24.

5 Ibid.

6 Alex Markels, "Turning the Tide at P&G," *U.S. News & World Report*, October 30, 2006, 69–71.

7 Lynn Andriani, "Workman, B&N, Fresh Direct: NYC Foodie Trifecta," *Publishers Weekly*. October 16, 2006, 8.

CHAPTER 22

1 Del Jones, "It's Lonely—and Thin-Skinned—at the Top," *USA Today*, January 16, 2007, 1B.

CHAPTER 23

1 Kate MacArthur, "Pepsi, Coke: We Satisfy Your 'Need States,'" *Advertising Age*, November 27, 2006, 3–23.

2 Mary Jane Credeur, "PepsiCo Net Rises 61% on Demand for Frito-Lay Snacks," *Bloomberg News*, Februrary 8, 2007.

3 Kate MacArthur, "Pepsi, Coke: We Satisfy Your 'Need States,'" *Advertising Age*, November 27, 2006, 3–23.

4 Stephanie Thompson, "Pepsi Dons Disguise in Attempt to Seduce the Whole Foods Devotees," *Advertising Age*, November 6, 2006.

5 Kate MacArthur, "Pepsi, Coke: We Satisfy Your 'Need States,'" *Advertising Age*, November 27, 2006, 3–23.

CHAPTER 24

1 Tom Benson, ed. "What Is Drag?" available at www.grc.nasa.gov/WWW/K-12/airplane/
   drag1.html (accessed April 27, 2007).

CHAPTER 25

1 Nanci Hellmich, "Most People Multitask, So Most People Don't Sit Down to Eat," *USA
   Today*, September 30, 2004.
2 *Consumer Reports on Health*, April 2006, Vol. 18 Issue 4, 10.
3 Claudia Wallis, Sonja Steptoe, and Wendy Cole, "Help! I've Lost My Focus!" *Time*, January 16, 2006, Vol. 167 Issue 3, p 72–79.
4 Ibid.
5 Ibid.
6 Katherine Rosman, "BlackBerry Orphans," *Wall Street Journal*, December 8, 2006.
7 Claudia Wallis, Sonja Steptoe, and Wendy Cole, "Help! I've Lost My Focus!" *Time*, January 16, 2006, Vol. 167 Issue 3, p 72–79.
8 Carol Kaufman-Scarborough and Jay D. Lindquist, *Time & Society*, September 2003, Vol.
   12 Issue 2/3, 350-370.
9 Ibid.
10 David H. Freedman, "Why interruption, distraction, and multitasking are not such awful
   things after all," *Inc.*; February 2007, Vol. 29 Issue 2, p 67–68, 2p.

CHAPTER 26

1 Claudia Wallis, Sonja Steptoe, and Wendy Cole, "Help! I've Lost My Focus!" *Time*, January 16, 2006, Vol. 167 Issue 3, p 72–79.
2 Ibid.
3 *Consumer Reports on Health*; April 2006, Vol. 18 Issue 4, 10.
4 Claudia Wallis, Wendy Cole, Sonja Steptoe, Sarah Sturmon Dale. "The Multitasking
   Generation," *Time*, March 27, 2006, Vol. 167 Issue 13, 48–55.
5 Ibid.
6 "Working round the clock," *The Week*, March 2, 2007, 36.

CHAPTER 27

1 Phil Britt, "The New Competitive Intelligence: Raising the Confidence Quotient,"
   KMWorld, November/December 2006, 11.
2 Ibid.

CHAPTER 31

1 Antony Bruno, "Console Wrap-Up," *Billboard*, December 23, 2006, Vol. 118 Issue 51, 20.
2 Catherine Colbert, "Nintendo Co. Ltd." Hoover's, accessed Feb. 22, 2007,
   http://www.hoovers.com/nintendo/--ID__41877--/freeuk-co-factsheet.xhtml.
3 Brian Bremner, "Nintendo Storms the Gaming World," Business Week Online, January
   29, 2007, 21, http://www.businessweek.com/globalbiz/content/jan2007/gb20070126_
   278776.htm?chan=globalbiz_asia_today's+top+story.
4 Jay Alabaster, "Nintendo's 9-Month Net Beats Full-Year Target," *The Wall Street Journal*,
   January 26, 2007.
5 James Surowiecki, "In Praise of Third Place," *The New Yorker*, December 4, 2006, Vol. 82
   Issue 40, 44.
6 Jay Alabaster, "Nintendo's 9-Month Net Beats Full-Year Target," *The Wall Street Journal*,
   January 26, 2007.
7 Aiko Wakao and Edwina Gibbs, "Nintendo sees profit doubling on strong DS sales,"
   Reuters News, January 9, 2007.

CHAPTER 32

1 Jennifer Reingold, "Rush Hour," Fast Company, November 2003, Issue 76, 67.
2 Ibid.
3 Tamara E. Holmes, "Hip-hop Couple a Cut Above the Rest," *Black Enterprise*, May 2004, Vol. 34
   Issue 10, 24.
4 Ellen McGirt, "Russell Simmons," *Money*, July 2004, Vol. 33 Issue 7, 45.

CHAPTER 33

1 Michael Arndt, "The New Face of Philips," Business Week Online, December 1, 2005, 20,
   http://www.businessweek.com/innovate/content/nov2005/id20051130_346148.htm.
2 Steve Lohr, "New Name and Strategy for Chip Division at Philips," *The New York Times*,
   September 1, 2006, C6.
3 David Armstrong, "Move into the Light," *Forbes*, August 14, 2006, Vol. 178 Issue 3,
   106–107.
4 Ibid.

CHAPTER 34

1 "How It Works," available at www.netflix.com/HowItWorks (Accessed January 24, 2006).
2 Netflix, "How It Works," available at www.netflix.com/HowItWorks (Accessed January 24,
   2006).
3 Michael Liedtke, "Netflix to Start Delivering Movies over the Internet," *Dallas Morning
   News*, January 16, 2007.

CHAPTER 36

1 Tyson Cole, in discussion with the editors, January 11, 2007.

Credits

*I*t's interesting reading the credits. You get to see who the author is. Who the author admires, connects with, appreciates, and thanks. You can even get a feeling for the size of the author's ego. You actually get to size up the author from a different angle than the book itself.

So here goes. Judge for yourself.

I published this book all by myself. Nobody helped and nobody deserves any credit but me. Now excuse me . . . I have to run to a mirror and admire myself.

. . . seriously now . . .

Although I am the author, I did not write this book without significant help and input from others. Leading the charge was my publisher and dear friend Meg La Borde. All who meet Meg love her. She is smart, fun, and has a keen eye for what makes sense in the confusing land of literary options. I took three runs at this book before finally coming up with the text you see here. Meg never flinched. She stayed dedicated and supportive, and she consistently went the extra mile. From countless emails sorting out details to late night debates about speed in our world to squeezing in last-minute conversations in a taxi dashing to my next engagement, Meg redefined the word *extraordinary*. Meg, thank you for helping make *The Age of Speed* what it is.

Working alongside Meg is considered the most honest guy in publishing, Ray Bard. Ray is more than a name behind the Bard label. I was most impressed and grateful for how personally involved he got in ramping the book up for its release. Thank you for taking such a personal interest in the book, Ray. You're a prince of a man!

Lari Bishop and Erin Nelsen deserve a massive debt of gratitude. They edited, researched, wrote, and interviewed with professionalism and enthusiasm. They took my words and made them shine. Lari and Erin worked around the clock for months to ensure their work was accurate and delivered in a timely manner. In addition I would like to thank Sheila Parr for the world-class interior design and Lisa Woods for her extraordinary cover design talents. Plus, muchos gracias to Jeff Morris and Tom Ehrenfeld for their editing genius and to Clint Greenleaf for his friendship and support. Moreover, the ten professional readers deserve a shout out. Your comments helped immensely. Thank you all for your creative abilities and expertise.

A couple of other partners providing the marketing muscle for *The Age of Speed* were Barbara Cave Henricks (publicist extraordinaire) and Mike Drew with Promote a Book. Barbara believed in this book from day one and was a pure joy to work with. Her expertise and contacts opened doors that I could never have done on my own. Mike's marketing mind repeatedly contributed to some fun and fruitful projects. Barbara and Mike, thank you very, very much for all your hard work!

Every level of delivering a book from inception to you holding it in your hands requires a champion, a person who carries the banner high. Believing in the book along with Ray, Meg, and me was Michael Sullivan at National Book Network. He is a man who cares a great deal and delivers on what he says he will do. Publishing can be a field of landmines, and Michael made for safe, expeditious passage through the highest ground. Michael, thank you for embracing *The Age of Speed* with such immediacy and fervor.

Cara Smith is my assistant and friend. If you can imagine the ideal coworker, it's Cara. She has boundless energy, dedication, loyalty, and expertise in managing a freewheeling author. I've told her many times, if she ever leaves me, I'm going with her. That goes for Karen Harris too. Karen is my agent for the speaking side of things. She is also a champion. Speakers' bureaus and meeting planners love her. Karen is one of the very best in the industry. Cara and Karen, I really can't say thank you enough for all that you do.

At this point, saying thank you to friends and family is far from sufficient. In fact, I recently learned that in the Quechuan language of Peru there is no such expression as "thank you." Instead, the mountain people of Peru have a culture of reciprocity. Thank you comes in the form of reciprocal acts.

You know who you are. Some of you gave ideas, offered to help in a multitude of ways, and gave an unconditional lending hand. I will not forget your kindness, and I can only hope that I can live up to the Quechua standard of reciprocity. You all inspire me to the highest standard of kindness and love.

Speaking of love, I will close with how much I cherish my wife and children. We have an unwritten contract concerning you, the reader. With my wife and kids' blessing, we share my time with you. The time it takes to travel to speeches and consulting is considerable. The writing sessions can impinge on family time, too. If you, the reader, were inclined to be grateful to anyone, it would be my children and, especially, my wife for making this happen. In a way you have already done this. You let the Quechua culture prevail and have honored my family by buying this book.

Michelle, Max, Alex, and Isabella, love is the highest form of thanks I can think of. You make our trip through the Age of Speed joyful and exciting. I love you!

Index

PHOTO: © GUY VIAU

Vince Poscente is best known for his ability to provide an invigorating message to organizations across the corporate landscape. Company leaders call on him to inspire employees to embrace speed when they feel compelled to resist it and to produce faster results in ways they find rewarding. When companies come face-to-face with speed, Poscente helps them understand the challenge and turn speed to their advantage.

To learn more about harnessing the power of speed, join the ever-increasing community of people who subscribe to Full Speed Ahead, a weekly eBrief that will help you discover how the force of speed can be put to use in your life and business.

www.vinceposcente.com